Mandingo Theory: Castration of Africans and Sex-crazed Conceptualization

By: Kofi Piesie

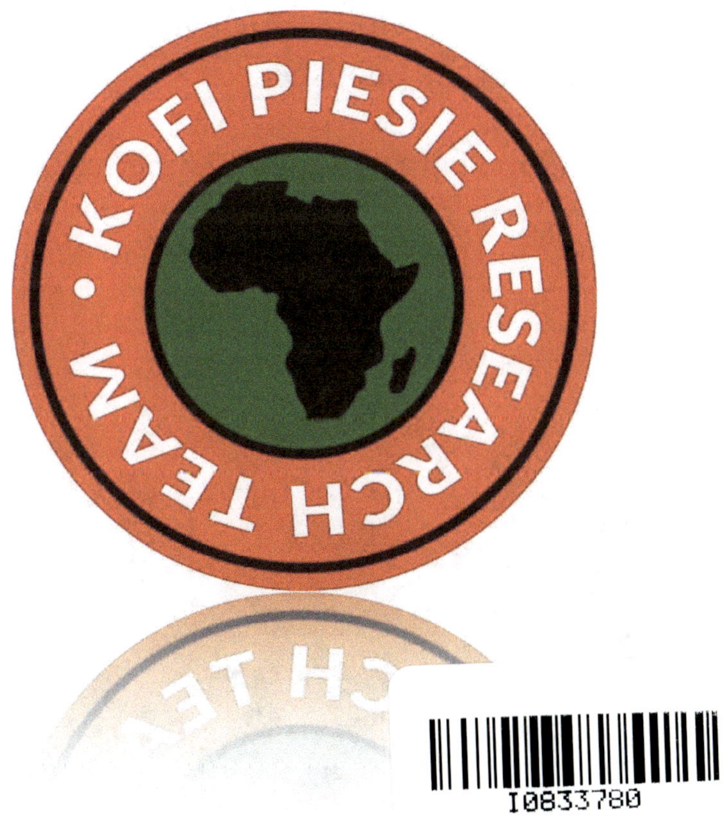

Kofi Piesie/Mossi Warrior Clan

Printed in the United States of America

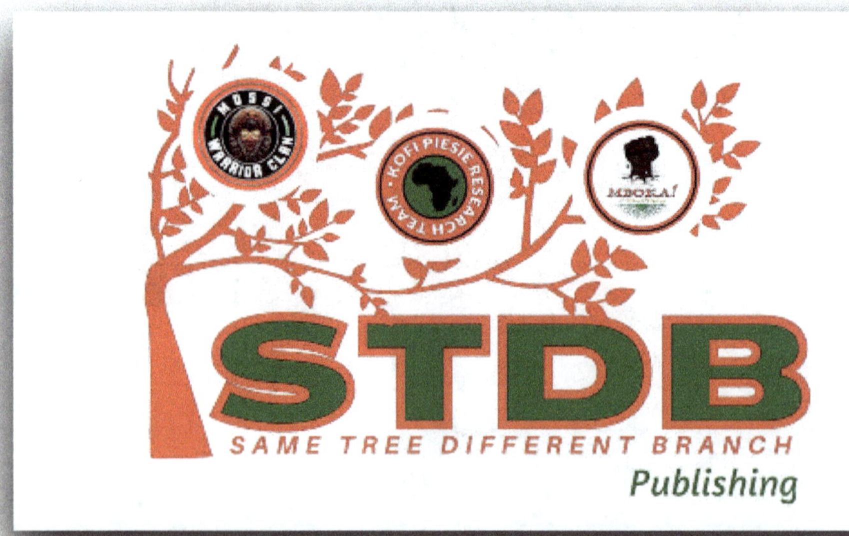

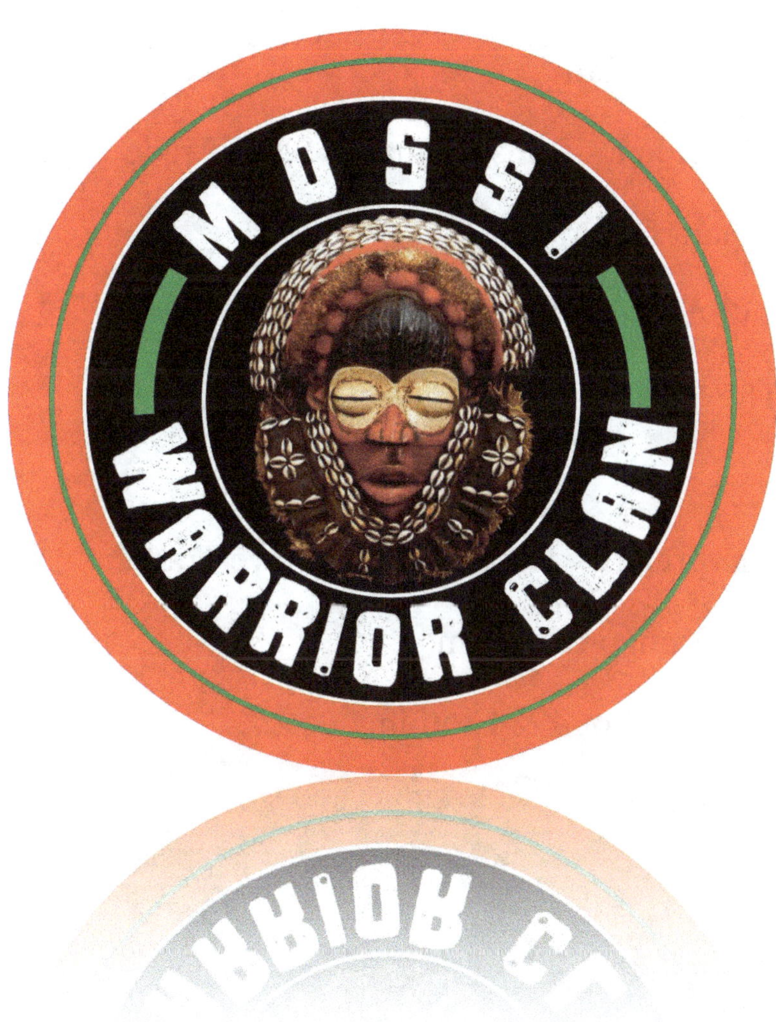
MOSSI
WARRIOR CLAN

Table of Content

Acknowledgement

First and foremost, I would like to thank my Ancestors who came before me. Jerreh len jeff suma ai maai mi contan si yen torop (Honor our Ancestors, and we respect you and are proud of the things you've done.

I have vowed to continue to build on the foundation of John Henrik Clarke, John G Jackson, Asa Hillard, Yosef Ben-Jochannan, Richard Wright, Chancellor Williams Amos N. Wilson, and Cheikh Anta Diop. I hope one day that I am spoken about in the same high regard as these great Ancestors.

I want to thank my wife for being understanding and not lashing out on me too much when I am up at all times of night reading, researching, and writing.

I also want to thank Kofi Piesie Research Team, who are my brothers and my friends. These men have pushed me to be great and have always been in my corner. Thanks, Mossi

Warrior Clan. I am grateful to be a part of this group and some of my brothers I honor you for inspiring me to work hard.

I hope those who read this book appreciate this work and those who have high expectations for me.

Introduction

Slavery is a heinous act and has existed for centuries. I do not condone anyone who has committed this crime. Some international seminars have been organized by scholars from universities, UNESCO, the Centre for Black and African Arts and Civilization, and other government agencies to examine the role of Arab merchants in the trans-Saharan slave trade, which lasted for 17 centuries. They also explore the role of the European powers in the trans-Saharan slave trade.

Papers presented at this seminar agreed that both slave trades were unprecedented in history and responsible for the deportation of millions of Africans to various parts of the world.

The participants also considered both slave trades to be crimes against humanity as defined by United Nations resolutions from the 2001 Durban conference on racism, racial discrimination, and xenophobia.

For decades, Nigerian representatives in UNESCO have urged member countries to examine the Atlantic and trans-Saharan slave trades as a critical reason for under-development in Africa.

Some of the seminar's participants affirmed that while the trans-Atlantic slave trade lasted for four centuries (1693-1884), the trans-Saharan slave trade continued for 17 centuries (652-1960). The Arabs still practice this crime called slavery after it was outlawed and no longer illegal.

Fatunde, Tunde. "Scholars Focus on the Arab Trans-Saharan Slave Trade." University World News, https://www.universityworldnews.com/post.php?story=20120413180645205.

In the woke community, the conscious community, and these YouTube streets, we have given the Arabs a pass, and we all skip the Trans-Sahara slave trade and talk about The European Trans- Atlantic slave trade. I get that the Europeans took slavery to a whole other level, but we must not forget what the Arabs did.

I was reading University World News, which comprises a network of some five dozen education journalists based in more than two dozen countries, with representation in all regions, states some Arab scholars, such as Ibn Khaldun, justified the trans-Saharan slave trade by interpreting some sections of the Koran that 'authorized' the enslavement of African' infidels' by Arab slave merchants, the 'chosen race.'

And some European scholars supported the trans-Atlantic slave trade by making copious references to the book of Genesis in the Bible. Consequently, slavery was not the product of racism. However, racism was one consequence of slavery.

The participants agreed that both slave routes were responsible for the migration of millions of Africans to other parts of the world. The statistics of deported Africans remain highly controversial among scholars.

One participant referred to the book Le Genocide Viole, written by the Senegalese historian and anthropologist Tidiane N'Diaye. They, using various sources, estimated that the trans-Atlantic slave trade deported some 20 million people while the trans-Saharan slave trade displaced around 10 million Africans.

Fatunde, Tunde. "Scholars Focus on the Arab Trans-Saharan Slave Trade." University World News, https://www.universityworldnews.com/post.php?story=20120413180645205.

Many numbers have been thrown out on how many Africans were kidnapped and displaced. In the above paragraph, historian and anthropologist Tidiane N'Diaye say 20 million Africans in the trans-Atlantic Slave Trade and around 10 million Africans were displaced in the Trans-Saharan slave trade. I have seen the numbers of displaced Africans as low as 12 or 12.5 million. Still, in my opinion, the numbers were way higher, even higher than historian and anthropologist Tidiane N'Diaye states, but we will never get the correct estimate of Africans kidnapped and displaced in the Tran-Saharan slave trade or Trans-Atlantic slave trade. I am not an expert, so I said in my opinion. Still, I know there are many dishonest intellectuals in those fields, such as history, anthropology, and paleontology.

I came across a pdf article from havard.edu that had information on how scholars came up with estimates of enslaved Africans that were taken. I will share some of this exciting information. On pages 6 – 8 of the pdf article entitled "Shackled to the past, "Nathan Nunn states that this chapter's analysis builds on a long empirical tradition in African history literature.

The seminal work is Philip Curtin's (1969) The Atlantic Slave Trade: A Census, which used data available to provide a detailed description and comprehensive analysis of the origins and destinations of slaves shipped during the trans-Atlantic slave trade. Since Curtin's publication in 1969, African historians have collected and analyzed an imposing amount of additional information.

The most recent and most extensive efforts are the Trans-Atlantic Slave Trade Database, which David Eltis developed, Stephen Behrendt, David Richardson, and Herbert Klein (1999), and the Louisiana Slave Database and the Louisiana Free Database, constructed by Gwendolyn Midlo Hall (2005). Another notable contribution to this literature is Patrick Manning's computer models to generate simulations of the estimated demographic impacts of Africa's slave trades. The results were presented in a series of journal articles and in his book Slavery and African Life, published in 1990.

The present analysis extends this line of research by using the available data to construct estimates of the number of slaves taken from the different parts of Africa. Then, the statistical relationship between the number of slaves taken in the past and the current economic performance is examined.

The data used to construct the slave export estimates can be grouped into two categories. The first category includes data that report the total number of slaves exported from each African port or region. The data for the trans-Atlantic slave trade is from the updated version of the Trans-Atlantic Slave Trade Database, which records 34,584 voyages from 1514 to 1866. These data are gathered from documents and records located around the world. In most European ports, merchants were required to register their ships, declare the volume and value of goods transported, pay duties, and obtain formal permission to leave the dock.

Therefore, for each vessel and voyage, typically, there exist many different registers and documents. In the database, 77% of the trans-Atlantic slave voyages after 1700 have shipping information from more than one source. Specific expeditions are documented in as many as sixteen different sources. The average number of sources of data for each voyage is six.

According to the authors' estimates, the database contains 82% of all trans-Atlantic slaving voyages ever attempted. The first purchase of slaves recorded in the Trans-Atlantic Slave Trade Database was in 1526, decades after the beginning of the trans-Atlantic slave trade. For this reason, Ivana Elbl's estimates of the number and locations of slaves shipped during the early period of the Atlantic slave trade are also used. Ivana Elbl's estimates, which cover the period from 1450 to 1521, are primarily based on volume estimates recorded by observers at the time and direct numerical data from surviving records.

Nunn, Nathan. Chapter 5. Shackled To The Past: The Causes And Consequences Of Africa's Slave Trades. Aug. 2008, https://scholar.harvard.edu/nunn/files/hup_africa_slave_trade10.pdf.

So, this is why I made the statement early that we will never get the correct estimate of Africans kidnapped and displaced in the Trans-Atlantic Slave Trade. They used two types of methods to "Estimate" how many African slaves were kidnapped: ethnicity data and shipping data.

During the Arab and European slave trade, some women slaves and males were castrated. Arabs castrated several male slaves and were a prominent feature of the trans-Saharan slave trade. The castrated male, called Eunuchs, were purchased by rich Arab kings and princes and employed as security agents to protect their harems.

In the European slave trade, castrations were used as a form of punishment because they were jealous of the African's enlarged private parts and wanted to show white dominance, which will be discussed in this book.

They both had their reasons why they castrated Africans, and I will attempt in each chapter to walk the reader through both sides and psychology behind many sex-crazed ideas that sparked the Mandingo theory and other theories that developed about the male and female private parts.

Table 5.1: Slave ethnicity data for the trans-Atlantic slave trade

Location	Time Period	Number of Ethnic Groups	Number of Slaves	Type of Document
Valencia, Spain	1482–1516	77	2,675	Crown Records
Puebla, Mexico	1540–1556	14	115	Notarial Records
Dominican Republic	1547–1591	26	22	Records of Sale
Peru	1548–1560	16	202	Records of Sale
Mexico	1549	12	80	Plantation Accounts
Peru	1560–1650	30	6,754	Notarial Records
Lima, Peru	1583–1589	15	288	Baptism Records
Colombia	1589–1607	9	19	Various Records
Mexico	1600–1699	28	102	Records of Sale
Dominican Republic	1610–1696	33	55	Government Records
Chile	1615	6	141	Sales Records
Lima, Peru	1630–1702	33	409	Parish Records
Rural Peru	1632	25	307	Parish Records
Lima, Peru	1640–1680	33	936	Marriage Records
Colombia	1635–1695	6	17	Slave Inventories
Guyane	1690	12	69	Plantation Records
Colombia	1716–1725	33	59	Government Records
French Louisiana	1717–1769	23	223	Notarial Records
Dominican Republic	1717–1827	11	15	Government Records
South Carolina	1732–1775	35	681	Runaway Notices
Colombia	1738–1778	11	100	Various Records
Spanish Louisiana	1770–1803	79	6,615	Notarial Records
St. Dominique	1771–1791	25	5,413	Sugar Plantations
Bahia, Brazil	1775–1815	14	581	Slave Lists
St. Dominique	1778–1791	36	1,280	Coffee Plantations
Guadeloupe	1788	8	45	Newspaper Reports
St. Dominique	1788–1790	21	1,297	Fugitive Slave Lists
Cuba	1791–1840	59	3,093	Slave Registers
St. Dominique	1796–1797	56	5,632	Plantation Inventories
American Louisiana	1804–1820	62	223	Notarial Records
Salvador, Brazil	1808–1842	6	456	Records of Manumission
Trinidad	1813	100	12,460	Slave Registers
St. Lucia	1815	62	2,333	Slave Registers
Bahia, Brazil	1816–1850	27	2,666	Slave Lists
St. Kitts	1817	48	2,887	Slave Registers
Senegal	1818	17	80	Captured Slave Ship
Berbice	1819	66	1,127	Slave Registers
Salvador, Brazil	1819–1836	12	871	Manumission Certificates
Salvador, Brazil	1820–1835	11	1,106	Probate Records
Sierra Leone	1821–1824	68	605	Child Registers
Rio de Janeiro, Brazil	1826–1837	31	772	Prison Records
Anguilla	1827	7	51	Slave Registers
Rio de Janeiro, Brazil	1830–1852	190	2,921	Free Africans' Records
Rio de Janeiro, Brazil	1833–1849	35	476	Death Certificates
Salvador, Brazil	1835	13	275	Court Records
Salvador, Brazil	1838–1848	7	202	Slave Registers
St. Louis/Goree, Senegal	1843–1848	21	189	Emancipated Slaves
Bakel, Senegal	1846	16	73	Sales Records
d'Agoué, Benin	1846–1885	11	70	Church Records
Sierra Leone	1848	132	12,425	Linguistic and British Census
Salvador, Brazil	1851–1884	8	363	Records of Manumission
Salvador, Brazil	1852–1888	7	269	Slave Registers
Cape Verde	1856	32	314	Slave Census
Kikoneh Island, Sierra Leone	1896–1897	11	185	Fugitive Slave Records

Table 5.2: Estimated slave exports from 1400 to 1900 by country.

Country name	Trans-Atlantic	Indian Ocean	Trans-Saharan	Red Sea	Total in all slave trades
Angola	3,607,402	0	0	0	3,607,402
Nigeria	1,410,970	0	555,796	59,337	2,026,102
Ghana	1,603,392	0	0	0	1,603,392
Ethiopia	0	200	813,899	633,357	1,447,455
Mali	524,031	0	509,950	0	1,033,981
Sudan	615	174	408,261	454,913	863,962
Dem. Rep. of Congo	759,270	7,047	0	0	766,317
Mozambique	382,378	243,484	0	0	625,862
Tanzania	10,834	523,992	0	0	534,826
Chad	823	0	409,368	118,673	528,862
Benin	454,099	0	0	0	454,099
Senegal	221,723	0	98,731	0	320,454
Togo	287,675	0	0	0	287,675
Guinea	242,529	0	0	0	242,529
Burkina Faso	183,101	0	0	0	183,101
Mauritania	419	0	164,017	0	164,436
Guinea-Bissau	156,084	0	0	0	156,084
Malawi	88,061	37,370	0	0	125,431
Madagascar	36,349	88,927	0	0	125,275
Republic of Congo	94,486	0	0	0	94,486
Kenya	303	12,306	60,351	13,490	86,448
Sierra Leone	69,377	0	0	0	69,377
Cameroon	62,405	0	0	0	62,405
Algeria	0	0	61,835	0	61,835
Ivory Coast	52,602	0	0	0	52,602
Somalia	0	229	26,194	5,855	32,277
Zambia	6,552	21,406	0	0	27,958
Gabon	27,393	0	0	0	27,393
Niger	150	0	0	19,779	19,929
Gambia	12,783	0	5,693	0	18,476
Libya	0	0	8,848	0	8,848
Liberia	6,794	0	0	0	6,794
Uganda	900	3,654	0	0	4,554
South Africa	1,944	87	0	0	2,031
Central African Rep.	2,010	0	0	0	2,010
Egypt	0	0	1,492	0	1,492
Zimbabwe	554	536	0	0	1,089
Namibia	194	0	0	0	194
Burundi	0	87	0	0	87
Equatorial Guinea	11	0	0	0	11
Djibouti	0	5	0	0	5
Botswana	0	0	0	0	0
Seychelles	0	0	0	0	0
Comoros	0	0	0	0	0
Swaziland	0	0	0	0	0
Rwanda	0	0	0	0	0
Sao Tome & Principe	0	0	0	0	0
Cape Verde Islands	0	0	0	0	0
Lesotho	0	0	0	0	0
Morocco	0	0	0	0	0
Mauritius	0	0	0	0	0
Tunisia	0	0	0	0	0

Chapter I
Trans-Saharan Slave Trade

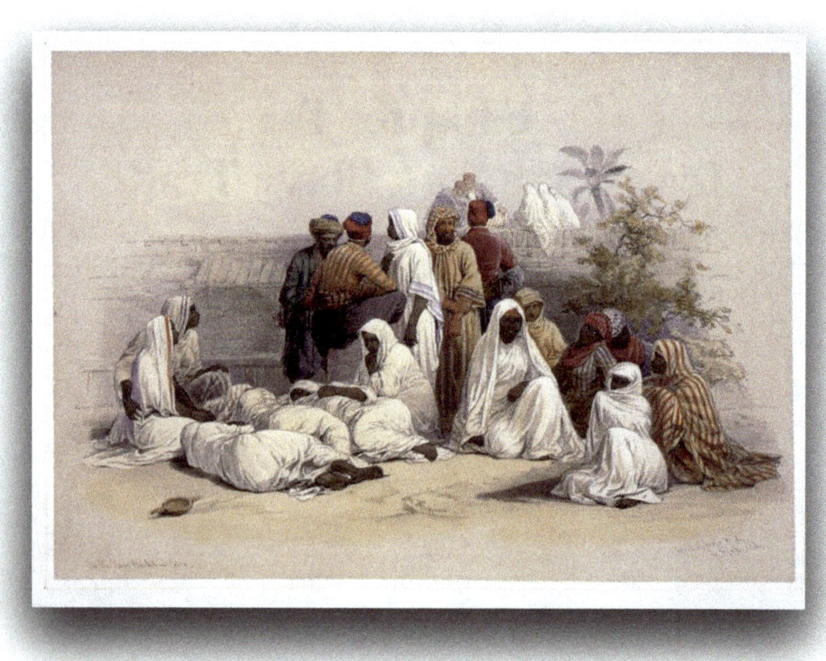

Trans -Sahara Slave Trade

Before we get into Trans-Saharan Slave Trade, let's first establish what the Sahara Desert is and understand its essential role in the Trans-Saharan Slave Trade; so I did a simple Wikipedia search but to make this clear, Wikipedia should be your first place to start but not your ending point, but because I am not trying to go too deep on Sahara desert, a quick search would do to get a basic understanding.

The direct source of the Wikipedia article stated that the Sahara is a desert on the African continent. With an area of 9,200,000 square kilometers (3,600,000 sq mi), it is the largest hot desert in the world and the third-largest desert overall, smaller only than the deserts of Antarctica and the northern Arctic.

Team, Esri's StoryMaps. "Is the World Full or Empty?" ArcGIS StoryMaps, Esri, June 16, 2022, https://storymaps.arcgis.com/stories/b4380439bc8c4293b36a4f9772c665ba.

The name "Sahara" is derived from the Arabic word for "desert" in the feminine irregular form, the singular ṣaḥra' (صحراء /ˈsˤaħra/), plural ṣaḥārā (صَحَارَى /ˈsˤaħaːraː/), ṣaḥār (صَحَار), ṣaḥrāwāt (صَحْرَاوَات), ṣaḥāriy (صَحَارِي).

al-Ba'labakkī, Rūḥī (2002). al-Mawrid: Qāmūs 'Arabī-Inklīzī (in Arabic) (16th ed.). Beirut: Dār al-'Ilm lil-Malāyīn. p. 689.

The desert comprises much of North Africa, excluding the fertile region on the Mediterranean Sea coast, the Atlas Mountains of the Maghreb, and the Nile Valley in Egypt and Sudan. It stretches from the Red Sea in the East and the Mediterranean in the North to the Atlantic Ocean in the West, where the landscape gradually changes from desert to coastal plains. To the South, it is bounded by the Sahel, a belt of semi-arid tropical savanna around the Niger River Valley and the Sudan region of sub-Saharan Africa.

The Sahara can be divided into several regions, including Western Sahara, the central Ahaggar Mountains, the Tibesti Mountains, the Aïr Mountains, the Ténéré desert, and the Libyan Desert.

For several hundred thousand years, the Sahara has alternated between desert and savanna grassland in a 20,000-year cycle caused by the precession of Earth's axis as it rotates around the Sun, which changes the location of the North African monsoon.

Chu, Jennifer (January 2, 2019). "A "pacemaker" for North African climate." MIT News. Retrieved January 20, 2020.

Sahara Desert Important Roll

From reading lots of material on the Trans-Saharan Slave Trade, those routes across the Sahara Desert were an essential part of the Arabs economies. Goods such as gold, salt, slaves, cloth, and ivory were transported across the desert using long trains of camels called caravans. The caravans would often travel in the evening or morning hours to avoid the heat of the day.

I mention gold, salt, slaves, clothes, and ivory, but I am only going to touch on salt, Berbers, camels, and their role; then, I will move into the Trans-Saharan Slave trade.

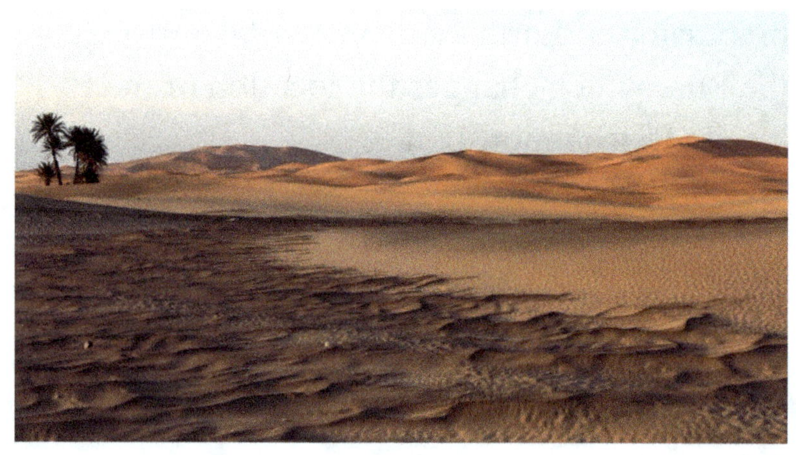

Salt A Major Trade Good

Salt from the Sahara Desert was one of the primary trade goods of ancient West Africa, where very few naturally occurring mineral deposits could be found—transported via camel caravans and by boat along such rivers as the Niger and Senegal. Salt found its way to trading centers like Koumbi Saleh, Niani, and Timbuktu, where it was either passed further South or exchanged for other goods such as ivory, hides, copper, iron, and cereals. The most common exchange was salt for gold dust from southern West Africa's mines. Indeed, salt was such a precious commodity that it was quite literally worth its weight in gold in some parts of West Africa.

Cartwright, Mark. "The Salt Trade of Ancient West Africa." World History Encyclopedia, Https:// Www.worldhistory.org#Organization, July 24, 2022, https://www.worldhistory.org/article/1342/the-salt-trade-of-ancient-west-africa/.

Camels The Ship of Desert

The trans-Saharan caravan trade was so dynamic and active that some historians call it a sandy sea. In other words, just like the Pacific and the Atlantic have trade routes with bustling ports, so did the Sahara. However, the trans-Saharan trade routes had sand and camels rather than water and ships. Camels were often called the ships of the desert.

They were the animal of choice mainly because they could carry lots of weight and go long periods without water. The fact that they could move relatively quickly was also a big plus. Traveling in large groups, these merchants and their camels formed caravans or groups of traders traveling long distances.

The Trans-Saharan Caravan Trade, Religion & Culture. (2015, March 5). Retrieved from https://study.com/academy/lesson/the-trans-saharan-caravan-trade-religion-culture.html.

So, you can see the Camels played a vital role in the Sahara Slave Trade network. If you study camels, you can see that these animals were well-adapted to life in the desert, which made it easy for the Arab to travel long distances across the Sahara Desert. I want to clarify one thing: even though the camel could travel long distances, many camels didn't make it, and those who didn't supply fresh meat.

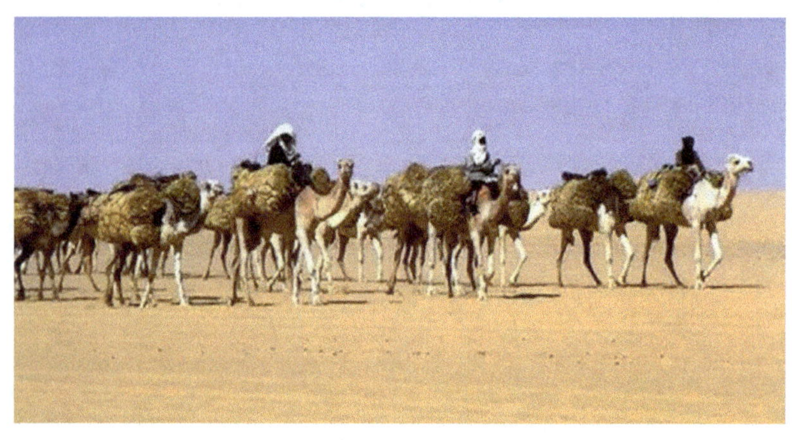

Trans-Saharan Camel Caravan

The salt of the Berbers was being brought from the Adrar by caravans, sometimes consisting of thousands of camels. A few years later, these Berbers were taking all the gold and cloth of the Upper Senegal (Galam) in exchange for their salt; presumably, slaves continued to feature in this commerce. By the mid-eighteenth century, powerful Saharans (the Awläd Mabarak) reportedly traded Ijil salt from Tishit to the Niger market of Segu in exchange for slaves and gold.

McDougall, Ann E. Slavery & Abolition: A Journal of Slave and Post-Slave Studies. n.d...

Informants told Richard Roberts in Segu that 'Moors' were the biggest purchasers of slaves in the region during the era of the slave-producing Segu-Bambara state (1712-1861).

In brief, the salt-slave relationship was one of great antiquity, and it was firmly rooted in the desert-side exchange networks controlled by Saharans.

McDougall, Ann E. Slavery & Abolition: A Journal of Slave and Post-Slave Studies. n.d.

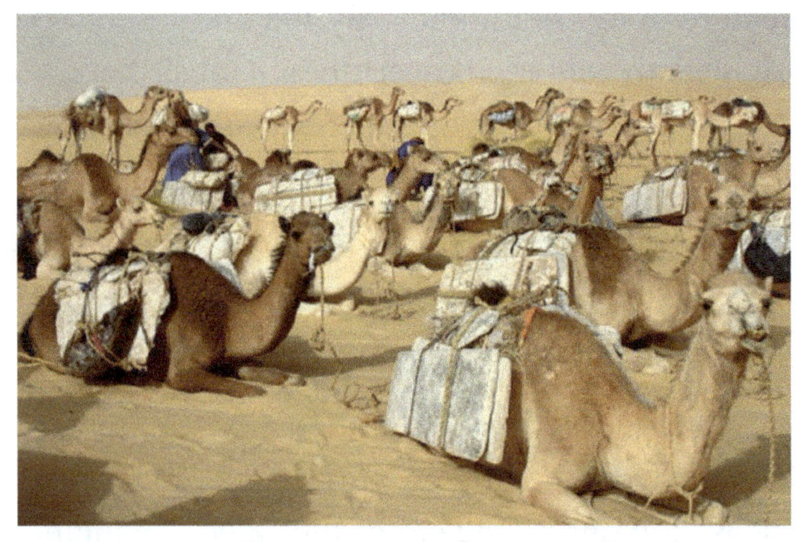

Image of camel's caravan operated by Berber nomads with salt in the Sahara Desert

The Trans-Saharan Slave Trade

Starting more than 700 years before the Trans-Atlantic Slave Trade, the Sub-Saharan Slave Trade, also known as the Arab Slave Trade, began in the late 7th century after the Arabs successfully defeated and took over Egypt and soon controlled North Africa, East Africa, and parts of West Africa such as Northern Senegal, Mali, Ivory Coast, and Nigeria.

Johnson, Elizabeth Ofosuah. "The Chilling Details of the Arab Slave Trade in Africa and the Barbaric Castration of Black Boys." Face2Face Africa, April 6, 2020, https://face2faceafrica.com/article/the-chilling-details-of-the-arab-slave-trade-in-africa-and-the-barbaric-castration-of-black-boys.

With complete control of a significant part of Africa, the Arabs began to capture young boys and girls. They took them to Egypt, where they were sold into slavery within Africa or carried across the Indian Ocean to Indonesia, China, Southwest Asia, and India.

By the tenth century, the demand for slaves from Africa to work as plantation hands, sex slaves, domestic maids, and slave warriors had significantly increased, so much so that an estimated number of 5000 slaves were shipped out of Africa a year, according to an article in the New African Magazine.

New African. "Recalling Africa's Harrowing Tale of Its First Slavers – The Arabs – as UK Slave Trade Abolition Is Commemorated." New African Magazine, March 27, 2018.

Similar to the Trans-Atlantic Slave Trade, captured slaves were beaten to be weakened and chained together; however, captured victims in the Sub-Saharan slave trade had to endure several weeks of walking through the desert carrying loads for their new masters from West or East Africa to Egypt or Zanzibar where they were eventually sold in the slave markets.

From my research early in the Trans-Saharan Slave Trade, more women were captured and were sex slaves. The women outnumbered the men, and the Arabs had numerous concubines. A concubine is a woman who lives with a man but has a lower status than his wife or wives. Today we have Viagra, Blue Chew, and a generic brand of Viagra called Sildenafil, and I wondered if they, in those times, had a plant that would give them the stamina to go and go. Some of these Arab men would have hundreds of concubines; that is a lot of pipe being laid.

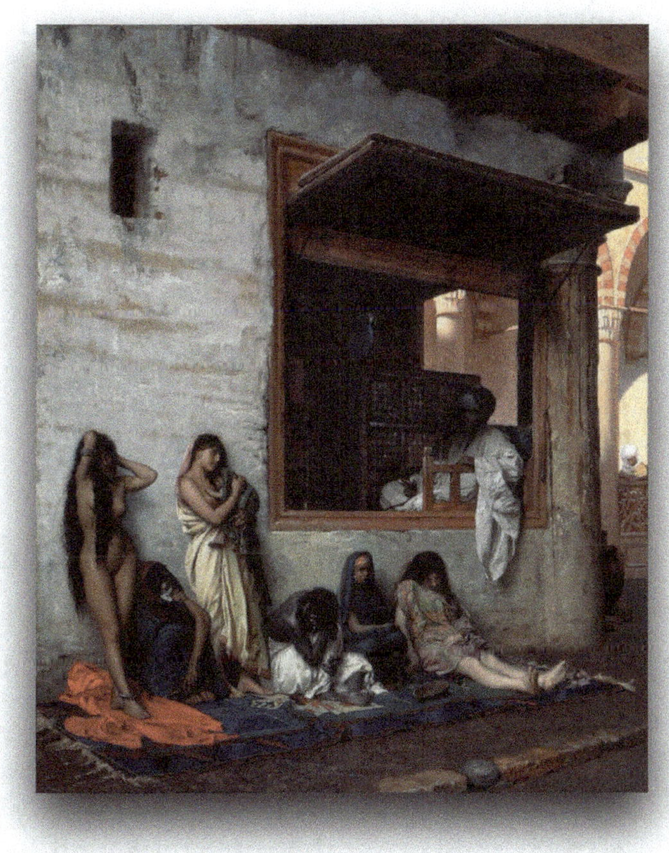

Looking at the image on the previous page, you can tell the Arabs enslaved everybody, such as the African, European, and Indians. Years ago, I read that Europeans would give or keep their women in the Arab slave trade. The European stating lower than a slave is their women. We can look through the historical record and see that it's not too far-fetched, seeing that they have constantly mistreated their women and never respected them.

According to Peter Preskar, who wrote The Horrific Medieval Slave Trade Had Gigantic (and Global) Proportions, said The Christian slaves were sold to the Muslims, the Muslim slaves to the Christians. The most desired were the pagan slaves. They could be sold to everyone.

For example, Roman Catholic Church forbade the enslavement of Catholics. However, it was completely fine to enslave Orthodox Christians and the rest of the non-Catholics.

• The famous Frankish king Charlemagne enslaved Slavs and sold them to the Muslims.

• The Byzantine Empire and the Arab Caliphates were the main markets for the slaves.

• The 11th-century Islamic invasions in India resulted in hundreds of thousands of Indians being enslaved.

Preskar, Peter. "The Horrific Medieval Slave Trade Had Gigantic (and Global) Proportions." Medium, History of Yesterday, March 8, 2022, https://historyofyesterday.com/medieval-slave-trade-410725bf9ffe.

I mentioned early that at the beginning of the Trans-Saharan Slave Trade, the Arabs had more women slaves than men. Still, by the 13th century, enslaved males were in higher demand because men could work longer and in several more areas than women. Now the price of a male slave was three times or more than that of a female slave. Due to religious beliefs, women were not allowed to work on plantations during their period, which affected productivity. It made them more valuable than only concubines and domestic workers.

Muslim slavery was not just economic; unlike the European slave trade, slavery in Islam was not wholly motivated by economics. Some Muslim slaves were used as productive labor, not generally on the same mass scale as in the West but in smaller agricultural enterprises, workshops, building, mining, and transport. Slaves were also taken for military service, some serving in elite corps essential to the ruler's control of the state, while others joined the equivalent of the civil service.

Another class in the Arab slave trade was castration, so the castration of male slaves soon became a practice among Arab slave traders because castrated boys were in higher demand. The Arabs thought the castration of men made them work faster, more efficiently, and more robust and were not a threat to slave masters and owners who feared that their wives, concubines, and female slaves would have affairs with them.

The castration process usually had the testicles of the young boys removed; however, in some extreme cases, the penis was cut off altogether.

At a point in time, in the slave trade, castrated boys were the most expensive on the market, and the death of one was a massive loss to the slave sellers or masters. Several died having to walk miles to slave markets where they were sold.

Ade, Yewande. "African Male Slaves Experienced Untold Hardship During the Slave Trade Era." History of Yesterday, July 10, 2021.

Castrated slave boys grew to become prestigious people in society at the time. Some joined the army or became Eunuchs, while others became a part of the royal court after serving royals for several years of their lives.

Ade, Yewande. "African Male Slaves Experienced Untold Hardship During the Slave Trade Era." History of Yesterday, July 10, 2021.

Okay, I know you say what a eunuch is. According to Ronald Segal, the Author of Islam's Black Slaves says, in Islam, castration is against the law. I don't think it was in the Koran; I think it was a hadith -- a saying attributed to the prophets which says he who castrates a slave will himself be castrated. But they got around this as people do. One contrivance was to buy already castrated slaves. Another was to employ those who were not Muslims to operate. But then, even these contrivances came to be abandoned, and dealers would perform the operation along the route. The mortality rates were huge.

Segal, Ronald. Islam's Black Slaves: A History of Africa's Other Black Diaspora. Atlantic Books, 2003.

To be technical, there was a crucial difference between white eunuchs and black eunuchs. Whites generally had only the testicles removed, whereas blacks underwent the most radical form, referred to as "level with the abdomen.

For reasons that are not altogether clear or explicit, they came to be used increasingly by rulers as counselors, advisors, and tutors and, eventually, to run the holy places of Mecca and Medina, where they were treated with enormous respect.

One can speculate on the motivation -- if they were not sexually active or preoccupied, they were more likely to be devoted and loyal or given to spiritual preoccupations instead of bodily ones.

Segal, Ronald. Islam's Black Slaves: A History of Africa's Other Black Diaspora. Atlantic Books, 2003.

Chapter II
Trans-Atlantic Trade Slave Trade

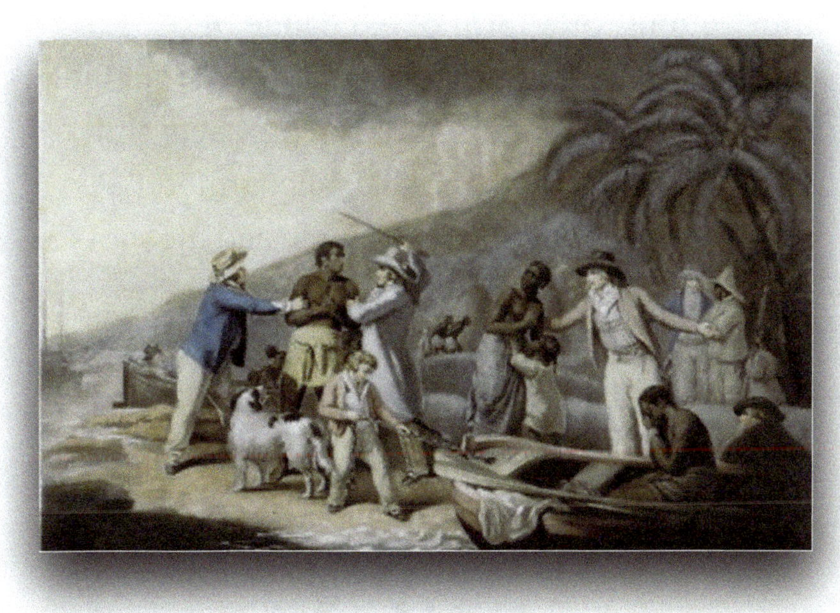

Trans-Atlantic Slave Trade

The Trans-Atlantic Slave Trade, also referred to as Triangle Slave Trade, revolved around transactions, or a form of exchange of importing and exporting commodities; we think of raw materials or agricultural products and goods, but Africans were also a commodity. Europeans took pots, pans, guns, and alcohol to Africa. Europeans, to African slaves to the Americans. Europeans took sugar, cotton, rum, tobacco, and coffee back to Europe.

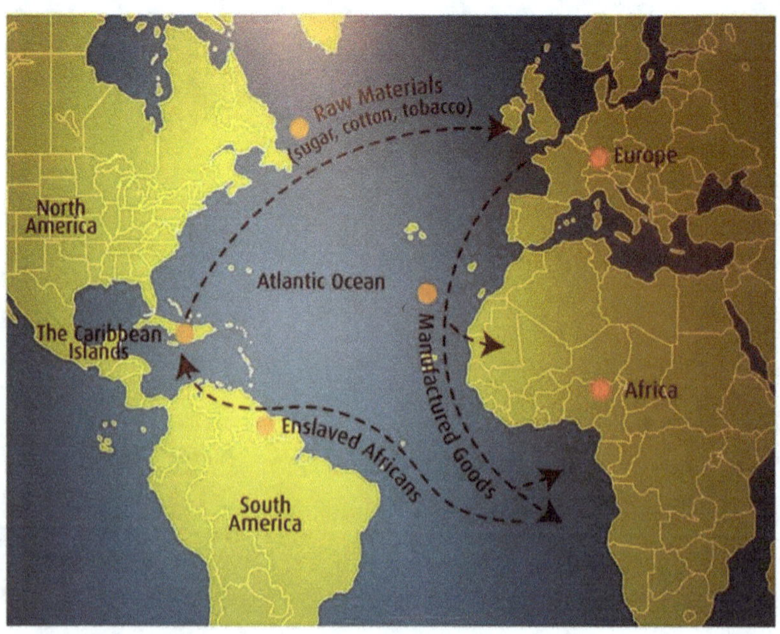

When discussing about the Trans-Atlantic Slave Trade, we have to talk about the Portuguese first, but before we get into that, I first want to say Trans-Atlantic Slave Trade was a non-humane and tragic experience for my Ancestors who were kidnaped, raped, beaten, and killed for no reason.

In the 1480s, Portuguese ships arrived in Central Africa at the mouth of the Congo River, the center of the Kongo kingdom. It was from the Kongo that Europeans got the name for the entire region. Initially, the Kongo was glad to trade with the Portuguese because the relationship provided a new market for their goods, and they received goods from the Portuguese. The Kongo also hoped that the Portuguese would share new technological knowledge.

In a few years, however, the Portuguese traders found that the Kongo could not supply the volume of gold, copper, and other valuable resources they wanted. After the Portuguese established sugar cane plantations on nearby islands off the coast of central Africa, they found African labor slaves to be a much more valuable commodity.

Curtis , Perry L., et al. Colonialism in the Congo: Conquest, Conflict, and Commerce. Choices Program, Watson Institute for International Studies, Brown University, 2007.

Slavery existed throughout the continent of Africa before Europeans began to travel there. In Africa, slaves were often prisoners of war captured from enemies, who were either eventually ransomed back to their families or sold to others. Frequently, enslaved people were allowed to earn money, own land, or even marry locals. Throughout generations, enslaved Africans and their descendants were often able to assimilate into their new societies.

In the Introduction of this book, I said I do not condone anyone who has committed this crime called slavery, so that also goes for Africans who, for whatever reason, did the same. I will touch on what slavery looked like in the Kongo later on in this chapter, but just reading the above paragraph, you should have a little understanding. Before I go any further, I would like to give a little history of the Kongo Kingdom.

The Kongo Kingdom

The Kingdom of the Kongo, also known as Kongo Day Ntotila or Wene Wa Kongo, also known as Wene Wa Kongois rank among the most famous kingdom in Sub-Saharan Africa. It is now Northern Angola, Cabinda, the Republic of the Congo, and the Western portion of the Democratic Republic of the Congo.

The empire consisted of six provinces ruled by a monarch, the ManiKongo of the BaKongo(Kongo) Peoples).

Kwekudee. "Pre-Colonial African Kingdom of Kongo: Once a Great Colosus." PRE-COLONIAL AFRICAN KINGDOM OF

KONGO: ONCE A GREAT COLOSUS, Blogger, 16 May 2013, https://kwekudee-tripdownmemorylane.blogspot.com/2013/05/pre-colonial-african-kingdom-of-kongo.html.

At its greatest extent, it reached from the Atlantic Ocean in the west to the Kwango River in the east and from the Congo River in the north to the Kwanza River in the south. The kingdom consisted of several core provinces ruled by the Manikongo, the Portuguese version of the Kongo title 'Mwene Kongo', meaning lord or ruler of the Kongo kingdom, but its sphere of influence extended to neighboring kingdoms, such as Ngoyo, Kakongo, Ndongo and Matamba.

Kwekudee. "Pre-Colonial African Kingdom of Kongo: Once a Great Colosus." PRE-COLONIAL AFRICAN KINGDOM OF KONGO: ONCE A GREAT COLOSUS, Blogger, 16 May 2013, https://kwekudee-tripdownmemorylane.blogspot.com/2013/05/pre-colonial-african-kingdom-of-kongo.html.

The founder chose this location because it offered the dual advantage of an almost central position in the kingdom and a natural defense against enemy attacks. Furthermore, on the plateau, according to Pigafetta (1591, Vol. I, p.

39), is the soil fertile, the air fresh, healthy, and pure; there are many springs of drinkable water which never hurts one's health, in any season. The abundance, the exceptional purity of the water, and the fertility of the land also struck a German traveler, Bastian (1859, pp. 123–5), in the nineteenth century. In O. Dapper's book (1668), there is a sketch drawn from memory that shows the capital erected on top of a cliff overlooking the Lunda River and the narrow valley.

Kwekudee. "Pre-Colonial African Kingdom of Kongo: Once a Great Colosus." PRE-COLONIAL AFRICAN KINGDOM OF KONGO: ONCE A GREAT COLOSUS, Blogger, 16 May 2013, https://kwekudee-tripdownmemorylane.blogspot.com/2013/05/pre-colonial-african-kingdom-of-kongo.html.

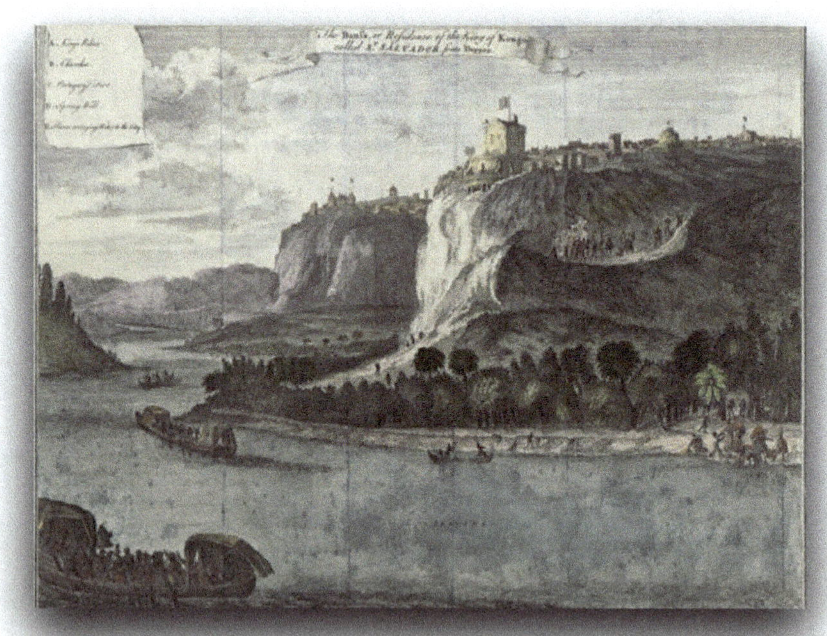

BANZA KONGO, Capital of the Kingdom of Kongo

When the Portuguese suggested trading merchandise for slaves, the concept among the Kongo and other peoples of the region was not new. However, the influence of the Portuguese and their high demand for slaves changed the local African societies. Conflicts between different groups intensified as they searched for new captives who could be traded for European manufactured goods, including weapons. The introduction of guns disrupted societies and changed the nature of their relationships. Those with direct contact with the Portuguese could trade humans for weapons which could then be used to capture still more slaves.

Nzinga Mbemba, who in most writing is known as King Alfonso was outspokenly disapproved of slavery and, in the beginning, fought the Portuguese demand for human beings; he eventually relented in order to sustain the economy of the Kongo. Initially, Nzinga Mbemba (King Alfonso) war captives and criminals in exchange to keep trading for Portuguese goods.

After Nzinga Mbemba (King Alfonso) gave in, and sometimes later, the Portuguese began to demand more and more slaves exceeding the country's potential supply prompting their search for slaves from neighboring regions. Ultimately the demand for slaves destabilized the Kongo. The Portuguese began to entice Bakongo people who didn't have much with goods, such as clothes, umbrellas, mirrors, and guns if they would capture the slave for them. The Portuguese also started beef with Bakongo People's neighbors, which war broke down their community or government, now making it easy to kidnap Central Africans

In 1514, the slave trade became an integral part of the economy of the area. Like all Kongo monarchs, Nzinga Mbemba (King Afonso) owned slaves, but he was troubled by the nature of this new slave trade. In 1526, he wrote to the Portuguese king about its disruptive effects on his kingdom; once he fully understood how the slave was being treated, he wanted it to stop. Remember, early, the BaKongo people did war with their kinsmen or neighbors, and those individuals became a prisoner of war, but these prisoners of war were not beaten, raped, are oppressed. They could roam freely and marry the Bakongo women, and once they worked off their debts, they could either integrate into the Bakongo society or return to their tribes, communities, and clans.

There is documentation or letters to the King of Portugal on how Nzinga Mbemba (King Alfonso) felt about what was happening to the prisoner of war and how criminals were being treated. Nzinga Mbemba (King Alfonso) also didn't like how his people were getting kidnapped and taken into slavery to be worked to death, beaten, killed, and raped. All this was reported to Portugal King as well.

The Portuguese jumped off everything and became a global sea power, and later, many European countries followed suit (Spain, Britain, France, United States, Denmark, and Sweden).

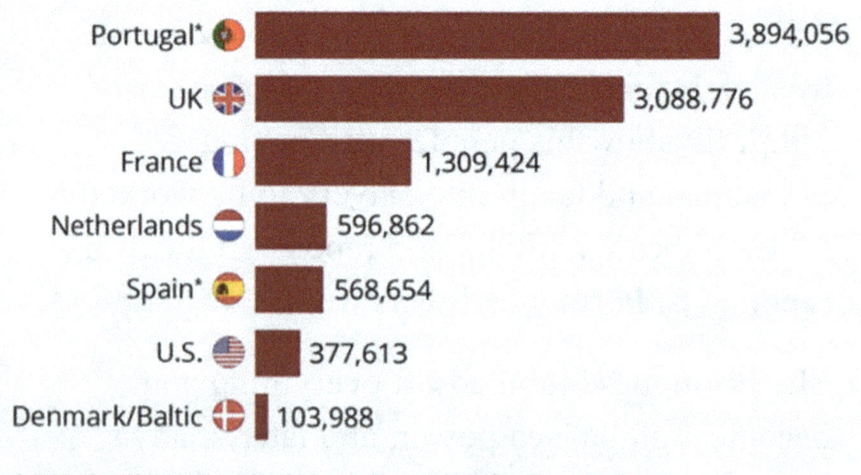
The Countries Most Active in the Trans-Atlantic Slave Trade
Number of enslaved Africans forced to embark on ships of the following national flags (1514-1866)
Portugal* 3,894,056
UK 3,088,776
France 1,309,424
Netherlands 596,862
Spain* 568,654
U.S. 377,613
Denmark/Baltic 103,988
* includes ships registered in country's Latin American colonies
Source: Slavevoyages.com

Author and scholar Joshua J. Mark writes Europeans shipped items to West Africa (the so-called First Passage) which then shipped enslaved humans to the Americas (the Middle Passage), and the Americas then shipped other items to Europe (Third Passage) and the whole circuit began again in a continuous cycle.

One of the more valuable items imported from Europe to West Africa was guns, shots, and gunpowder which African tribes could purchase through trade in human beings. A tribe with guns could subdue another, sell them into slavery for more guns, and expand their territory. Although this arrangement seemed to empower the Africans, it only profited the European slavers, who received more and more people as slaves.

Okay, you see this tactic with all European countries; they bring gun powder, guns, and goods into Africa and give them to some Africans within that society to kidnap their brethren or neighbors.

We also see within the historical record these Europeans give rival tribes guns. After the tribes went to war, they swooped in and take more slave to facilitate what they needed to be done on those plantations.

In The Trans Saharan Slave Trade, the Arabs had camels to travel and hold cargo across the Sahara Dessert. Still, in the Trans-Atlantic Slave Trade, the Europeans had ships to travel and carry cargo across the Atlantic Ocean.

The slaves were packed tightly in the hold of the ship, men chained and separated from women, boys separated from the rest. They were forced to lie on their sides to save space and were given small buckets to relieve themselves which many could not reach, and too small for the numbers below deck to be of any use anyway. As they made their way across the Atlantic on the Middle Passage, they were allowed above deck in good weather, chained to prevent any leaping overboard.

Once the ship reached the Americas, the slaves were unloaded into pens, cleaned and clothed (they had been brought naked unless a captain ordered them covered), and sold to the colonists.

Mark, Joshua J. "African Slave Life in Colonial British America." World History Encyclopedia, Https://Www.worldhistory.org#Organization, 27 July 2022, https://www.worldhistory.org/article/1732/african-slave-life-in-colonial-british-america/.

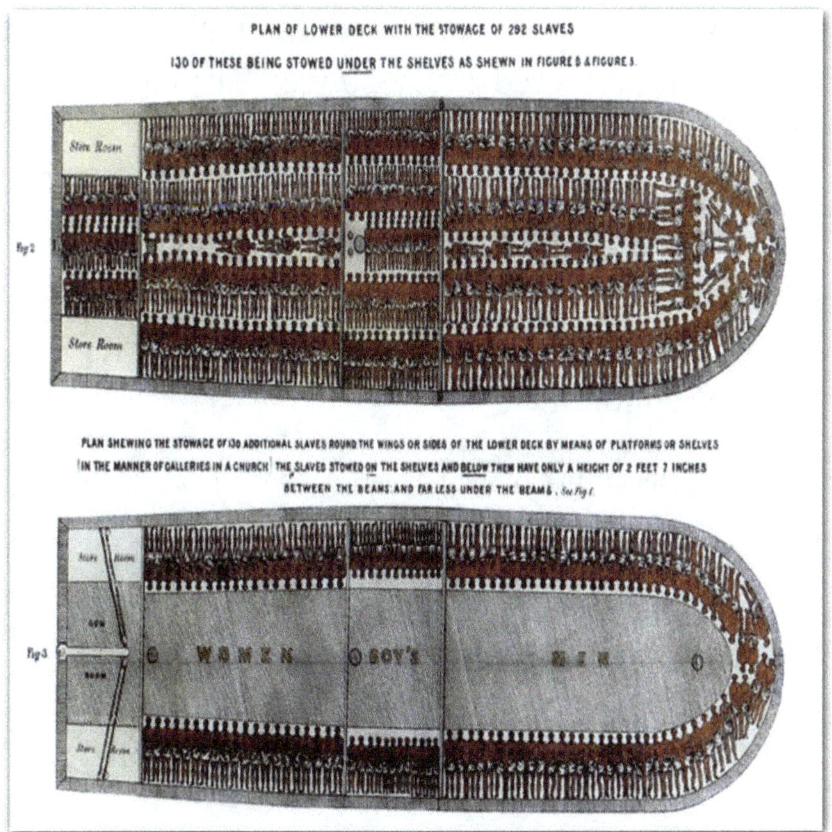

Housing, Food & Clothing

The life of a slave differed between colonies and, within communities, from master to master. Colonists in the New England and Middle colonies often had slaves living in their homes or a small shack on the land, while those in the Southern Colonies had numerous buildings known as slave quarters. Reiss describes a typical slave shack:

It was a one-room frame dwelling with a dirt floor that measured 17 by 20 feet. The cabin had at least one glazed and shuttered window. There was one door with a plate stock lock and a brick chimney with a dirt-floored brick hearth. This provided accommodations for seven or eight adults, with perhaps a sleeping loft for children.

Reiss, O. Blacks in Colonial America. McFarland, 2006.

Other cabins were built of logs and had no windows and no door – only a cloth or fur over the doorway – with a fireplace and chimney. There was no furniture, little light, and spaces between logs let in rain or snow.

Reiss, O. Blacks in Colonial America. McFarland, 2006.

In New England, the Puritans took better care of their slaves than the plantation owners of the south because they adhered more closely to the biblical example of slaves in the Old Testament who ate and slept with the family. In the Middle Colonies, slaves were fed primarily on corn and yams, which were distributed on Sunday, while, in the south, rice was the staple food.

Taylor, A. American Colonies: The Settling of North America. Penguin Books, 2002.

Clothing was also provided by the master and varied in quality depending on how much he chose to spend. The clothing of one's slaves could be, but was not always, a sign of one's wealth and status. So-called "house negroes" who tended children, cooked, cleaned, and served as butlers were always well-clothed as were slaves who regularly accompanied their masters into town. In the Southern Colonies, plantation slaves went nearly naked for most of the year, both men and women wearing little more than a loin cloth.

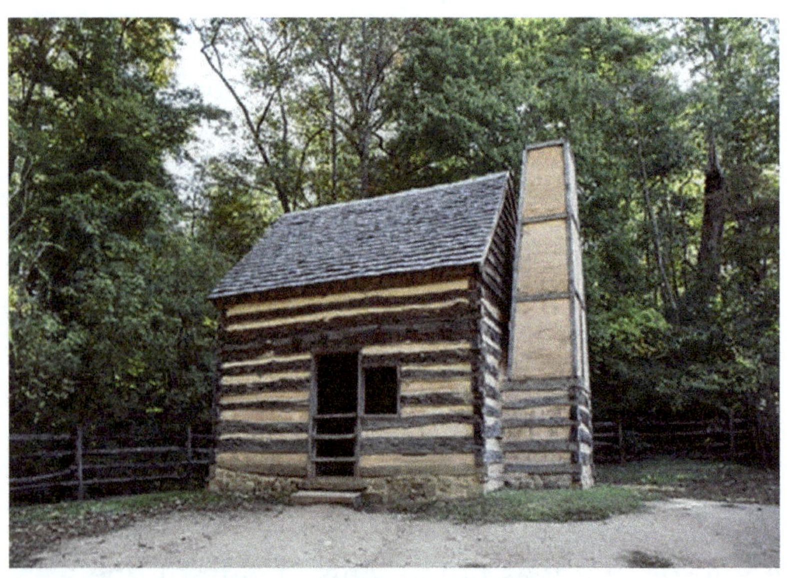

Slave Quarters

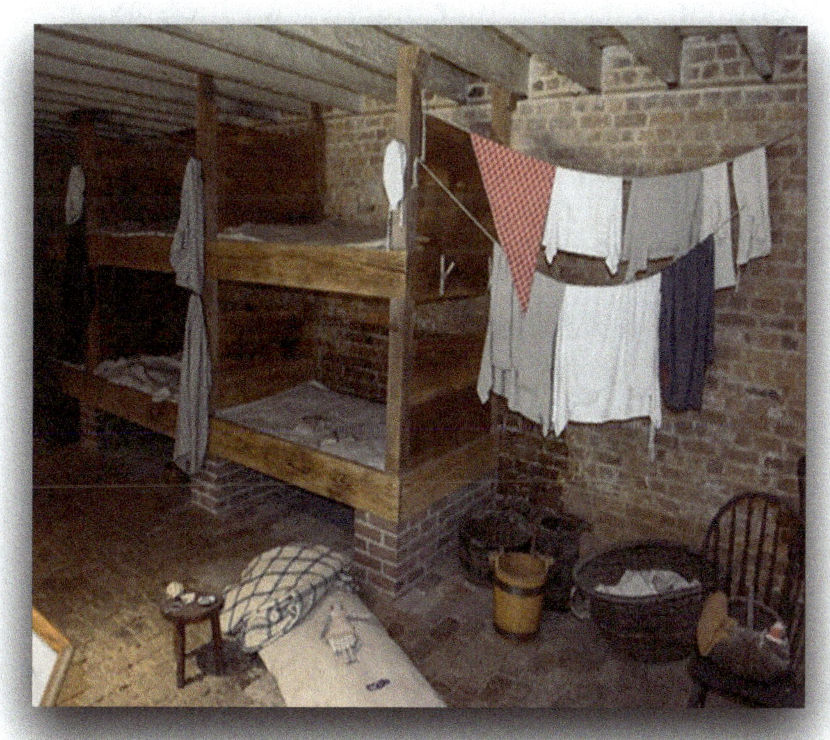

Inside the Slave Quarter

Castration

Castration was a form of punishment; male slaves were either castrated or mutilated. It was done to take away any iota of male pride that they had and to show the white man's dominance as a regular practice for the slave traders because it was believed that castrated boys and men worked faster, were more efficient, and posed no threat. The slave masters could leave them with their families without any fear that they would have affairs with their wives back at home.

Just like the Arabs, the Europeans believed castrating boys and men would make them work faster; however, it gets deeper for the European where they developed the psychology of paranoia, jealousy, hatred, and many sexual theories about the African sexual nature and enlarge private parts of African Men. I will talk about these theories and sexual abuse in chapter four.

Castration involved the removal of the testicles, and in extreme cases, the penis was cut off altogether. The main targets were young boys between the ages of 9 to 12. Sadly, many boys lost their lives to the horrendous process because it was brutal.

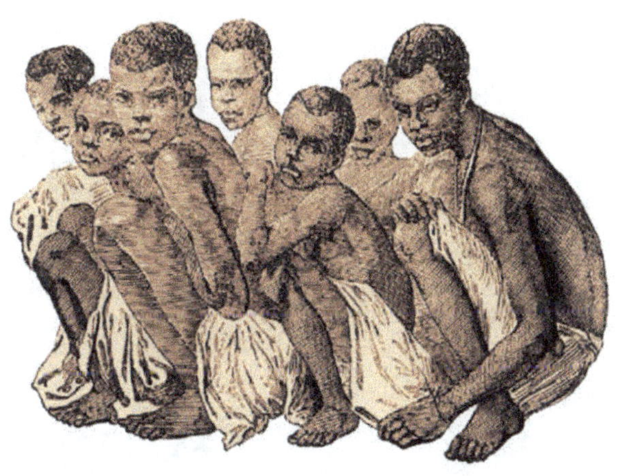

Castrated young boys between the ages of 9 to 12

Chapter III
Castration

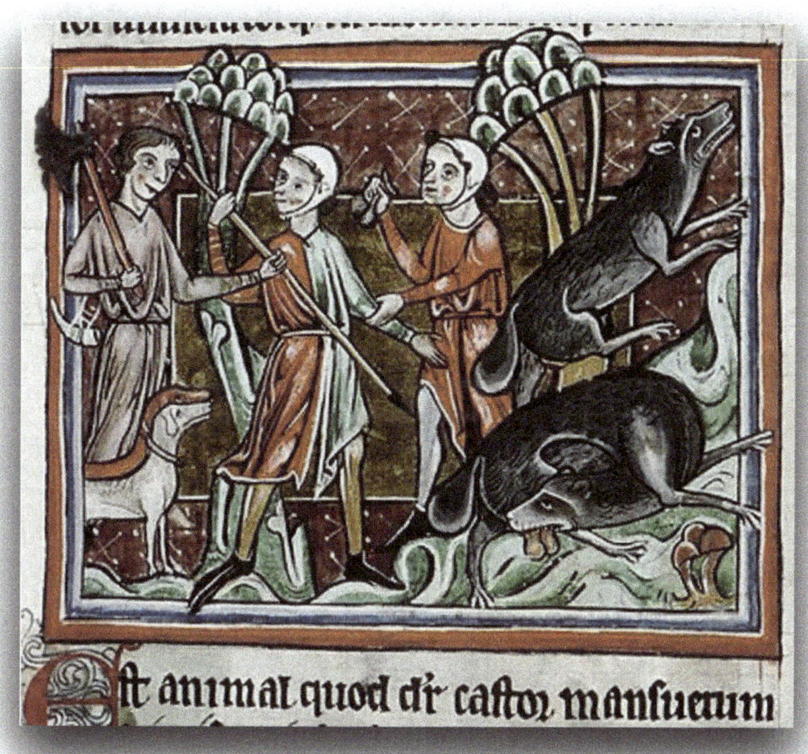

Castration

At the end of the last chapter, we briefly touch on castration, and in this chapter, I will go further into the effects, origin, and practice of castration. Hopefully, at the end of this chapter, we will better understand this horrible practice.

The word “castration” has often been traced back to a Mediaeval myth about beavers, whose Latin name is castor. Beavers were hunted to harvest sweet-smelling “castoreum” from scent glands near the root of the penis. Purportedly, a cornered beaver would bite off its scrotum and toss it to its pursuers to end the hunt. But there is a significant flaw in this story because beavers, as in many other water-living mammals, but in contrast to primates, the testes do not descend but remain in the belly cavity. So, there is no scrotum to bite off!

The dangling scent glands at the penis base have often been misreported as the beaver’s testes.

(Martin, Robert D. Unmanned: An Unnatural History of Human Castration. Sussex Publishers, 2016.)

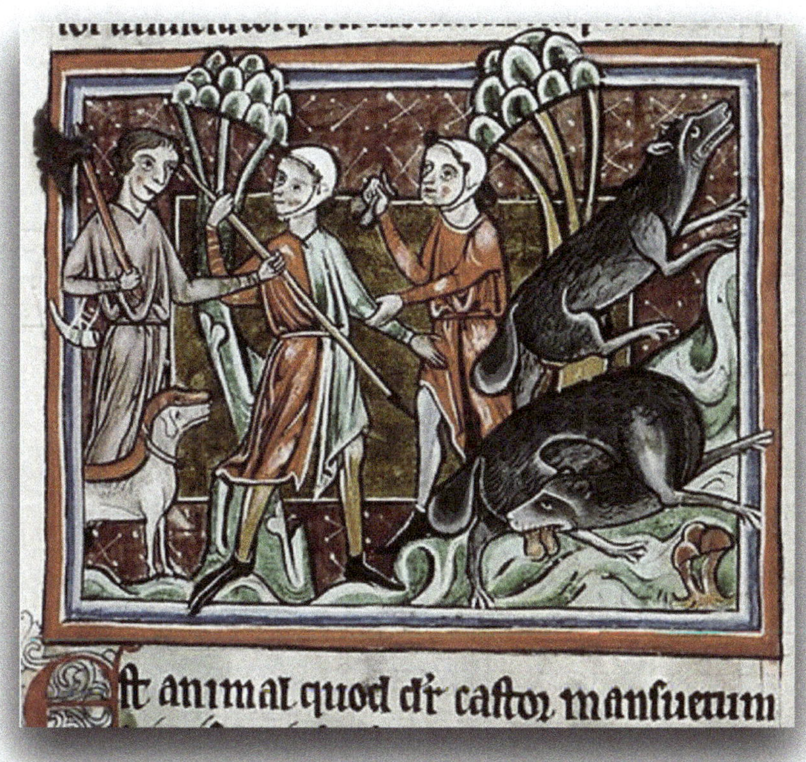

Castration

At the end of the last chapter, we briefly touch on castration, and in this chapter, I will go further into the effects, origin, and practice of castration. Hopefully, at the end of this chapter, we will better understand this horrible practice.

The word "castration" has often been traced back to a Mediaeval myth about beavers, whose Latin name is castor. Beavers were hunted to harvest sweet-smelling "castoreum" from scent glands near the root of the penis. Purportedly, a cornered beaver would bite off its scrotum and toss it to its pursuers to end the hunt. But there is a significant flaw in this story because beavers, as in many other water-living mammals, but in contrast to primates, the testes do not descend but remain in the belly cavity. So, there is no scrotum to bite off!

The dangling scent glands at the penis base have often been misreported as the beaver's testes.

(Martin, Robert D. Unmanned: An Unnatural History of Human Castration. Sussex Publishers, 2016.)

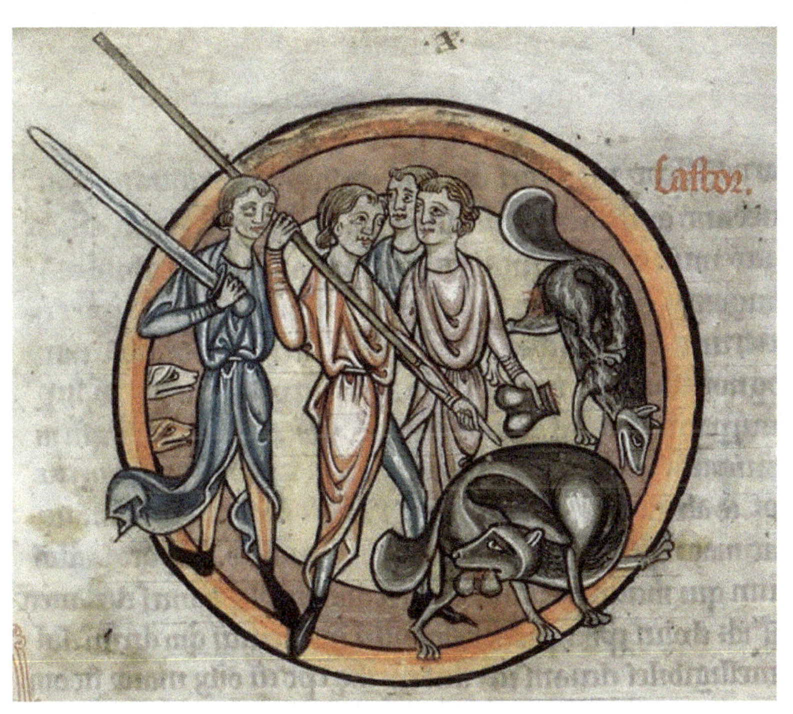

WHAT IS CASTOREUM?

Castoreum is a substance secreted by male and female Alaskan, Canadian, and Siberian beavers from pouchlike sacs near the base of their tails (castor is the word for beaver in Latin).

Beavers can't see or hear very well, but they have a great sense of smell, and due to their castoreum glands, they also smell great. They use their castoreum in part to mark their territory, secreting it on top of mounds of dirt they construct on the edges of their home turf. (The castoreum squirting out is so loud, you can hear it if you're standing nearby.) Beavers also use fatty, waxy secretion to waterproof their fur.

Lohman, Sarah. "A Brief History of Castoreum, the Beaver Butt Secretion Used as Flavoring." Mental Floss, Mental Floss, 13 June 2017, https://www.mentalfloss.com/article/501813/brief-history-castoreum-beaver-butt-secretion-used-flavoring.

An odorous combination of vanilla and raspberry with floral hints, castoreum carries information about a beaver's health and helps to make distinctions between family members and outsiders. Beavers are so interested in the smell that historically, fur trappers would bait traps with castoreum.

Lohman, Sarah. "A Brief History of Castoreum, the Beaver Butt Secretion Used as Flavoring." Mental Floss, Mental Floss, 13 June 2017, https://www.mentalfloss.com/article/501813/brief-history-castoreum-beaver-butt-secretion-used-flavoring.

It is said that castoreum is fresh; it's a fluid that ranges in color from yellow and milky to grey and sticky, depending on the type of beaver and its gender. In a live animal, this fluid is milked and dried to a solid for perfume making. In a dead animal, the entire castoreum gland is removed and, traditionally, preserved by smoking it over a wood fire.

Animal writer and natural world writer Rachel Poliquin states in her book "Beaver" that castoreum was used as a medicine for much of its history. Roman women inhaled the fumes of castoreum burned in lamps because they believed it would induce abortions (it didn't). Hildegard von Bingen, a 12th-century Benedictine abbess, mystic, and scholar, wrote that powdered beaver "testicles" drunk in wine would reduce a fever; the castoreum gland, when dried, is easily mistaken for testes. Castoreum has also been used to treat headaches, which makes sense given that it contains salicylic acid, the main ingredient in aspirin.

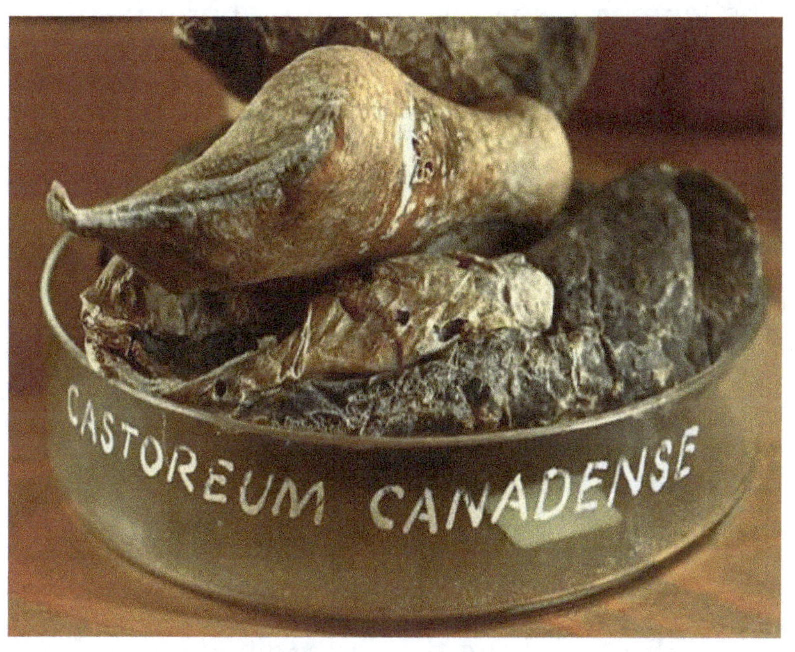

Dried castoreum on display in a museum

Origin

The temporal, spatial, and cultural origins of castration, both animal and human, are currently unclear, though there has been much speculation, at least regarding human castration. The motivation for animal castration has always been ascribed to herd and breeding control, especially for wool herds and draught animals. Still, scholars have propounded several hypotheses about the motivation for the development of human castration. These include but are not limited to punishment, control, disposal of potential rivals for power, medical 'cures,' and the deliberate creation of particular slaves and servants. A combination of these factors likely led to the widespread use of castration throughout history; however, the antiquity of the practice and the general abhorrence for and reluctance to be associated with the creation of castrates, but not the utilization of castrates, has led to millennia of cultural obfuscation and denial, making it especially difficult to pinpoint castration's origins.

Additionally, language has further confused the issue, as there are several ongoing linguistic debates about whether certain words mean "castrate" or merely "court official."

(Hopkins, 1978; Kadish, 1969; Ringrose, 1994; Siddall, 2007; Tadmor, 1983)

No single place of origin or single motivation for castration may have existed. It may have arisen in multiple locations for various reasons within a given period of time and gradually spread to surrounding cultures. It seems that the origins of animal and human castration may be linked, as the first references to human castrates (in the cult of Ishtar in Uruk) appear about the same time (circa 4000 B.C.) that animal herds, primarily sheep and goats, began to be intensively maintained and improved.

Davis suggested a possible underlying reason for the origin of castration when he stated that domestication is a move to control nature rather than to take from it. This is particularly relevant to the exploitation of secondary animal products as a further step in the domestication of animals, as part of the process of herd maintenance is controlling which members of the herd are viable breeders. This control is more manageable in males because the gonads are external. Since females bear the young, keeping as many of them as possible in the viable breeding population while restricting which males are part of that same breeding population allows for controlled herd increase.

(Reusch, Kathryn. That Which Was Missing: The Archaeology of Castration. University of Oxford, 2013.)

As castrating male sheep serves as a herd breeding strategy that prevents the loss of herd numbers while additionally improving wool quality, it is possible that wool herders quickly learned the benefits of castration. The concept of controlling breeding rights and abilities in a population readily transfers to human people, as evidenced by the practice of individuals or families deliberately choosing certain marriage partners.

Whether animal castration (and perhaps human castration) came before or after the large-scale domestication of animals for secondary products is currently unclear but is a topic worth pursuing. The sudden increase in the human population and the subsequent specialization and urbanization of specific groups of people post-neolithic and secondary products revolution may have prompted the intensification of both human and animal castration.

Later practices, such as the castration of the children of rebel leaders in the Ming Dynasty, had led to the speculation that in the early periods of castration history, when individuals who were foreign or otherwise 'other' were absorbed into a group through slavery, conquest, or some other mechanism, it may have been thought that these individuals must be controlled and, in some cases, perhaps prevented from interbreeding with the native population.

It may have been thought that the best way to control the genetic makeup of the total population was to remove any chance for breeding, something that could be easily practiced on individuals with few to no rights. Herd improvement techniques may then have been applied to disobedient slaves or prisoners of war to make them more tractable.

(Reusch, Kathryn. That Which Was Missing: The Archaeology of Castration. University of Oxford, 2013.)

Human Castration

There are two main types of human castration recorded in texts from the Roman period to the present day: the removal or destruction of only the testicles or the complete removal of both the testicles and the penis.

(Klaf and Pisetsky, 1962; Millant, 1908)

In this chapter, the removal of only the testicles will be referred to as partial castration, and the removal of both the penis and the testicles will be called complete castration. However, medically both methods are considered complete castration, as both involve the complete ablation of the testicles.

The type of castration employed seemingly depended on the area where the castration was performed, with complete castration generally used in Africa, the southern portion of the Near

East, India, South Central Asia, and China, and the complete removal of the testicles used in Europe, the northern part of the Near East, including Anatolia, and northern Central Asia.

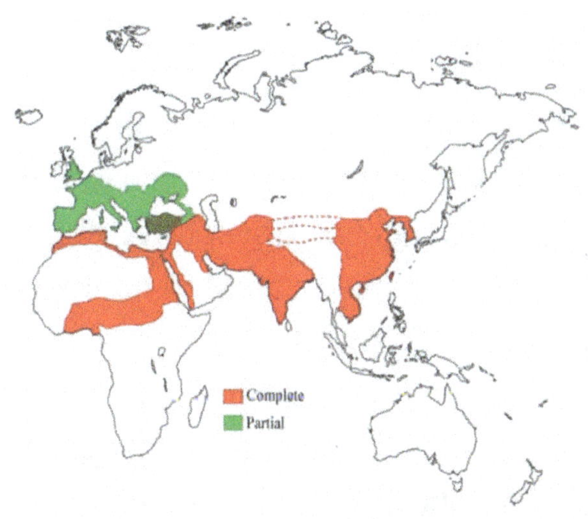

Most of the cultures which regularly employed castrates were empires, leading to Hopkins and Patterson's hypotheses about the nature of the castrate/ruler relationship, which they called imperial eunuchism. The reasons for castration varied greatly from region to region, place to place, time to time, and culture to culture.

(Reusch, Kathryn. That Which Was Missing: The Archaeology of Castration. University of Oxford, 2013.)

I found this interesting from my brief research that men castrated themselves because they could not feed their families, boys sought financial gain or steady employment, and slavers sought financial gain from selling castrated slaves. Vast categories encompass personal reasons for castration, but each person who chose to be castrated had a unique motivation behind their castration.

Castration as a judicial punishment requires further clarification as it both was not used as a method of supplying castrates for imperial uses. There are several law codes from across Afro-Eurasia which made castration a punishment for a range of transgressions, including rape, civil disobedience, rebellion, and adultery.

(Kadish, 1969; Kutcher, 2010; Scholz, 2001; Tougher, 2008)

Additionally, castration could be chosen in China to avoid the death penalty, as demonstrated by the Chinese historian Sima Qian. Whether these individuals, once castrated, were used within the imperial system or were allowed to return to their former lives seems to have depended on the time and place in which they were castrated. However, Qian continued his career as a historian and bureaucrat; the children of rebels in the Ming and Qing dynasties, who had been castrated so as not to continue their rebellious parents' lineages, were employed in the palace as servants. Whether this can be considered a form of slavery is debatable.

(Sima, Qian, et al. War-Lords. Southside, 1976.)

What we know of human castration today is not highly discussed in the academic setting; however, due to a particular interest in archeology, studies have begun to uncover more fruitful data regarding regions that participate in the practice. Those areas with cultures that heavily employed castrates will have the most likelihood of producing skeletons and other material cultures related too castration. It is possible that castration in humans on a wide scale first occurred in Uruk, Sumer, around 4000 B.C., in relation to the cult of the goddess Ishtar.

(Taylor, 2002)

Eunuchs may have been employed in the Assyrian Empire, mainly at the court. They could fulfill roles as diverse as personal attendant, administrative and military official, servant or professional. (Tougher, 2008)

Finding references to castrates in Assyrian documents is somewhat problematic, as there is some linguistic debate as to the actual meaning of the term šareši, which is generally taken to mean eunuch (castrate) but which could instead mean only court official. A similar problem affects the interpretation of the presence of castrates in dynastic Egypt. There are laws referring to castration as a method of punishment in dynastic Egypt, but it seems unlikely that there were large numbers of castrates in Egypt until the arrival of the Persian and Hellenistic dynasties.

(Kadish, 1969; Scholz, 2001; Tougher, 2008)

The use of castrates in Assyria may have influenced their employment in the Achaemenid Dynasty of Persia (550-330 B.C.), widely referenced by the Greeks, and somewhat born out through Persian documentation. The Achaemenid, Parthian (238 B.C.-A.D. 236), and Sassanid (A.D. 205-651) Persian dynasties influenced the Greek and Roman worlds through trade and direct contact. The Classical Greeks (500-323 B.C.) were not great consumers of castrates, but they may have been willing to take advantage of the wealth that could be gained by selling castrates to the Persians if an anecdote in Herodotus is to be believed. The spread of eunuchism across the Hellenistic world (323-31 B.C.) may have stemmed from the influence of Persia on the newly formed empire of Alexander the ~~Great~~ Greek.

Alexander the ~~Great~~'s Greek conquest of Persia and the subsequent fracturing of Alexander's empire into four kingdoms may have introduced and promoted the presence of castrates across the majority of the Hellenistic world, though eunuchs most likely became common features only at the Ptolemaic (305-30 B.C.) and Seleucid (312-63 B.C.) courts.

(Reusch, Kathryn. That Which Was Missing: The Archaeology of Castration. University of Oxford, 2013.)

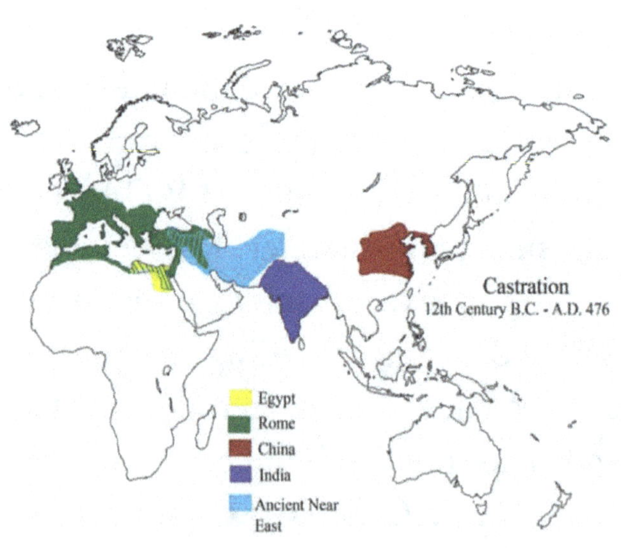

As we can see, castration has been practiced in the ancient world for different reasons, such as control, punishment, to separate strong stock away from weak stock, for crimes including rape, civil disobedience, rebellion, and adultery, and men castrating their selves because they were unable to feed their families. The Sumerians, the Romans, the Persians, the Greeks, the Egyptians, and China were practitioners of castrations.

When getting to the Arab Trans Saharan Slave Trade and The Europeans Trans-Atlantic Slave Trade, they had a foundation to build on. Scholars and historians believe it started with animals first and later with humans, but there is no scholarly consensus on where castration originated.

Chapter IV
Slave Breeding/Sexual Abuse

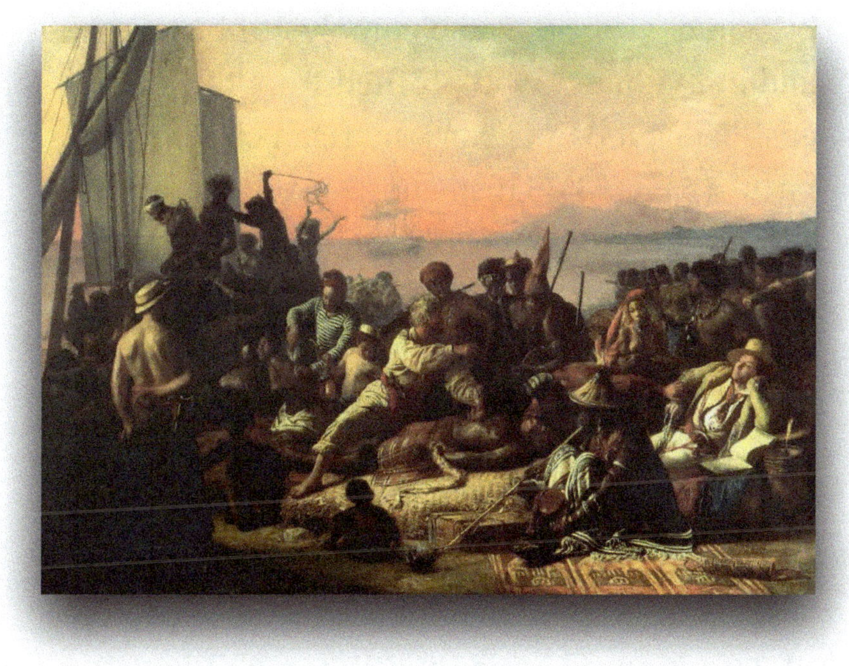

Slave Breeding/Sexual Abuse

There is no consensus as to what constitutes slave breeding. The Sublettes define the slave-breeding industry as the complex of businesses and individuals "who profited from the enslavement of African American children at birth" (page 13). This is not a useful definition. Presumably, all slaveholders profited from the enslavement of African American children at birth (otherwise, they would have manumitted them). Indeed, using their definition, all slaveholders could be classified as slave breeders. Most scholars define slave breeding as the use of barnyard techniques normally associated with animal husbandry. The choice of definitions is important. When Phillips writes that there is "no shred of supporting evidence" of slave breeding, he implicitly adopts the more widely accepted definition. Kenneth Stampp The Peculiar Institution (Vintage, 1956), p. 245 agrees that "evidence of systematic slave breeding is scarce. But if the term is not used with unreasonable literalness, if it means more than owner-coerced mating, numerous shreds of evidence exist which indicate that slaves were reared with an eye to their marketability—that the domestic slave trade was not 'purely casual.'" The choice of definition affects the amount of evidence of slave breeding.

Sublette, Ned, and Constance Sublette . American Slave Coast: A History of The Slave-Breeding Industry. CHICAGO REVIEW, 2017.

No one knows how many slaveholders bred slaves for the market. Abolitionists accused slaveholders of breeding slaves for sale, and slaveholders vehemently denied it. Contemporary tourists in the South wrote about slave breeding, but none observed it. Stamp suggests that slaveholders did not record such practices because of its objectionable nature. Of course, the lack of documentation may also indicate that relatively few slaveholders bred slaves for sale. Regardless, the scarcity of documented cases makes it difficult to substantiate the authors' claims.

Consider, for example, their statement that "the southern economy depended on the functioning of a slave breeding industry" (p. 3). Because the number of slave breeders is unknown, one can only speculate about the state of the southern economy in the absence of such an industry.

Sublette, Ned, and Constance Sublette . American Slave Coast: A History of The Slave-Breeding Industry. CHICAGO REVIEW, 2017.

From what we just read, those writers say there is little evidence or little evidence of slaveholders breeding other slaves. We know that slaveholders and those who policed the plantation coerced mating and mated strong slaves with other strong slaves. I will let those kidnapped Africans speak for themselves and tell us about breeding and sexual abuse by their so-called slave masters. Each narrative will be from a different African experience on the plantation. Remember when you read the transcribed interviews of once fugitives and ex-slaves, it may look incorrect or funny, but that is exactly how they spoke.

For many enslaved African Americans, one of the cruelest hardships they endured was sexual abuse by the slaveholders, overseers, and other white men and women whose power to dominate them was complete. Enslaved women were forced to submit to their masters' sexual advances, perhaps bearing children who would engender the rage of a master's wife and from whom they might be separated forever. Masters forcibly paired "good breeders" to produce strong children they could sell at a high price. Resistance brought severe punishment, often death. "I know these facts will seem too awful to relate," warns former slave William J. Anderson in his 1857 narrative, ". . . as they are some of the real 'dark deeds of American Slavery." On Slaveholders' Sexual Abuse of Slaves Selections from 19th- & 20th-century Slave Narratives.

National Humanities Center on the Masters' Sexual Abuse of Slaves: Selections from 19th- & 20th-c. Slave Narratives

Presented here are selections from multiple narratives: 19th-century memoirs of fugitive slaves, often published by abolitionist societies, and the 20th-century interviews of former slaves compiled in the 1930s by the Works Progress Administration (WPA) Slave Narrative Project (reproduced here as transcribed by the interviewers).

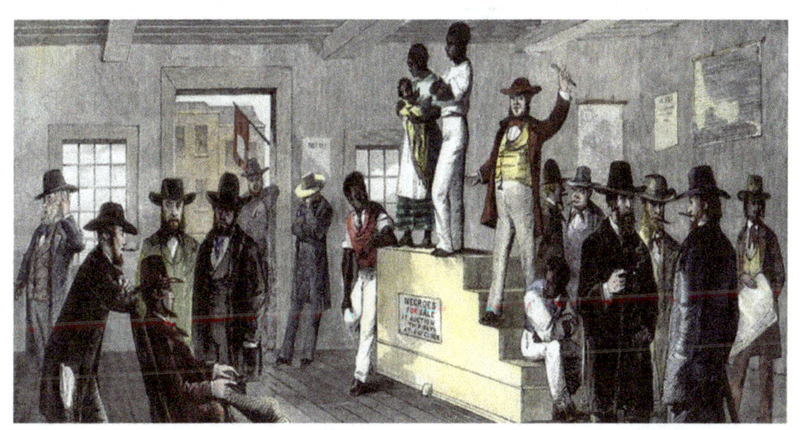

Slave Narrative

Dere am one thing Massa Hawkins does to me what I can't shunt from my mind. I knows he don't do it for meanness, but I allus [always] holds it' gainst him. What he done am force me to live with dat nigger, Rufus,' gainst my wants.

After I been at he place 'bout a year, de massa come to me and say, "You gwine live with Rufus in dat cabin over yonder. Go fix it for livin'." I's 'bout sixteen-year-old and has no larnin', and I's jus' igno'mus chile. I's thought dat him mean for me to tend de cabin for Rufus and some other niggers. Well, dat am start de pestigation for me.

I's took charge of de cabin after work am done and fixes supper. Now, I don't like dat Rufus, 'cause he a bully. He am big and 'cause he so, he think everybody do what him say. We'uns has supper, den I goes here and dere talkin', till I's ready for sleep and den I gits in de bunk. After I's in, dat nigger come and crawl in de bunk with me' fore I knows it. I says, "What you means, you fool nigger!" He say for me to hush de mouth. "Dis em my bunk, too," he say.

"You's teched in de head. Git out," I's told him, and I puts de feet' gainst him and give him a shove, and out he go on de floor' fore he know what I's doin'. Dat nigger jump up, and he mad. He look like de wild boar. He starts for de bunk, and I jumps quick for de poker. It am 'bout three foot long, and when he comes at me, I lets him have it over de head. Did dat nigger stop in he tracks! I's say he did. He looks at me steady for a minute, and you's could tell he thinkin' hard. Den he go and set on de bench and say, "Jus wait. You thinks it am smart, but you's am foolish in de head. Dey's gwine larn you somethin.'

"Hush yous big mouth and stay' way from dis nigger, dat all I wants," I say, and jus' sets and hold dat poker in de hand. He jus' sets, lookin' like de bull. Dere we'uns sets and sets for 'bout an hour and den he go out and I bars de door.

De nex' day I goes to de missy [mistress: master's wife] and tells her what Rufus wants, and missy say dat am de massa's wishes. She say, "Yous am de portly gal, and Rufus am de portly man. De massa wants you-uns for to bring forth portly chillen.

I's thinkin' 'bout what de missy say, but say to myse'f, "I's not gwine live with dat Rufus." Dat night when him come in de cabin, I grabs de poker and sits on de bench and says, "Git' way from me, nigger,' fore I busts yous brains out and stomp on dem." He say nothin' and git out.

De nex' day de massa call me and tell me, "Woman, I's pay big money for you and I's done dat for de cause I wants yous to raise me chillens. I's put yous to live with Rufus for dat purpose. Now, if you doesn't want whippin' at de stake, yous do what I wants."

I thinks 'bout massa buyin' me offen de [auction] block and savin' me from bein' sep'rated from my folks and 'bout bein' whipped at de stake. Dere it am. What am I's to do? So I' cides to do as de massa wish and so I yields.

I never marries, 'cause one' sperience am 'nough for dis nigger. After what I does for de massa, I's never wants no truck with any man. De Lawd forgive dis cullud woman, but he have to 'scuse me and look for some others for to' plenish de earth.

ROSE WILLIAMS, enslaved in Texas, interviewed ca. 1937 [WPA Slave Narrative Project]

My master often went to the house, got drunk, and then came out to the field to whip, cut, slash, curse, swear, beat and knock down several for the smallest offense or nothing at all.

He divested a poor female slave of all-wearing apparel, tied her down to stakes, and whipped her with a handsaw until he broke it over her naked body. In process of time, he ravished her person and became the father of a child by her. Besides, he always kept a colored Miss in the house with him. This is another curse of Slavery — concubinage and illegitimate connections, which is carried on to an alarming extent in the far South. A poor slave man who lives close by his wife is permitted to visit her but very seldom, and other men, both white and colored, cohabit with her. It is undoubtedly the worst place of incest and bigamy in the world. A white man thinks nothing of putting a colored man out to carry the fore row [front row in field work] and carry on the same sport with the colored man's wife at the same time.

I know these facts will seem too awful to relate, but I am constrained to write of such revolting deeds, as they are some of the real "dark deeds of American Slavery." Then, kind reader, pursue my narrative, remembering that I give no fiction in my details of horrid scenes. Nay, believe, with me, that the half can never be told of the misery the poor slaves are still suffering in this so-called land of freedom.

WILLIAM J. ANDERSON, Life and Narrative of William J. Anderson, Twenty-Four Years a Slave, 1857

I knew a man at the South who had six children by a colored slave. Then there was a fuss between him and his wife, and he sold all the children but the oldest slave daughter. Afterward, he had a child by this daughter and sold mother and child before the birth. This was nearly forty years ago. Such things are done frequently in the South. One brother sells the other: I have seen that done.

WILLIAM THOMPSON, enslaved in Virginia, interviewed in Ontario, Canada, 1855; in Benjamin Drew, The Refugee: Or the Narratives of Fugitive Slaves in Canada, 1856

[Patsey] had a genial and pleasant temper and was faithful and obedient. Naturally, she was a joyous creature, a laughing, light-hearted girl rejoicing in the mere sense of existence. Yet Patsey wept oftener and suffered more than any of her companions. She had been literally excoriated. Her back bore the scars of a thousand stripes — not because she was backward in her work, nor because she was of an unmindful and rebellious spirit, but because it had fallen to her lot to bc the slave of a licentious master and a jealous mistress.

She shrank before the lustful eye of the one and was in danger even of her life at the hands of the other, and between the two, she was indeed accursed.

In the great house, for days together, there were high and angry words, poutings, and estrangement, whereof she was the innocent cause. Nothing delighted the mistress so much as to see her suffer, and more than once, when Epps had refused to sell her, has she tempted me with bribes to put her secretly to death and bury her body in some lonely place in the margin of the swamp. Gladly would Patsey have appeased this unforgiving spirit if it had been in her power, but not like Joseph, dared she escape from Master Epps, leaving her garment in his hand.

Patsey walked under a cloud. If she uttered a word in opposition to her master's will, the lash was resorted to at once to bring her to subjection.

If she was not watchful when about her cabin or when walking in the yard, a billet of wood or a broken bottle, perhaps, hurled from her mistress' hand, would smite her unexpectedly in the face. The enslaved victim of lust and hate, Patsey had no comfort of her life.

SOLOMON NORTHUP, Twelve Years a Slave: Narrative of Solomon Northup, 1853

I was born in North Carolina, in Caswell County; I am not able to tell in what month or year. What I shall now relate is what was told me by my mother and grandmother. A few months before I was born, my father married my mother's young mistress. As soon as my father's wife heard of my birth, she sent onc of my mother's sisters to see whether I was white or black, and when my aunt had seen me, she returned back as soon as she could and told her mistress that I was white and resembled Mr. Roper very much.

Mr. Roper's wife, not being pleased with this report, she got a large club-stick and knife and hastened to the place in which my mother was confined. She went into my mother's room with a full intention to murder me with her knife and club, but as she was going to stick the knife into me, my grandmother happening to come in, caught the knife, and saved my life. But as well as I can recollect from what my mother told me, my father sold her and myself soon after her confinement [period of seclusion after childbirth].

MOSES ROPER, Narrative of the Adventures and Escape of Moses Roper, from American Slavery, 1840

There is no legal marriage among the slaves of the South. I never saw nor heard of such a thing in my life, and I have been through seven of the slave states. A slave marrying according to law is a thing unknown in the history of American Slavery. And be it known to the disgrace of our country that every slaveholder, who is the keeper of a number of slaves of both sexes, is also the keeper of a house or houses of ill-fame.

Licentious white men can and do enter at night or day the lodging places of slaves, break up the bonds of affection in families, destroy all their domestic and social union for life; and the laws of the country afford them no protection.

HENRY BIBB, Narratives of the Life and Adventures of Henry Bibb, An American Slave, 1849

There was a whisper that my master was my father, yet it was only a whisper, and I cannot say that I ever gave it credence. Indeed, I now have reason to think he was not.

Nevertheless, the fact remains, in all its glaring odiousness, that, by the laws of slavery, children in all cases are reduced to the condition of their mothers. This arrangement admits of the greatest license to brutal slaveholders and their profligate sons, brothers, relations, and friends and gives to the pleasure of sin the additional attraction of profit. A whole volume might be written on this single feature of slavery, as I have observed it.

One might imagine that the children of such connections would fare better in the hands of their masters than other slaves. The rule is quite the other way, and a very little reflection will satisfy the reader that such is the case. A man who will enslave his own blood may not be safely relied on for magnanimity. Men do not love those who remind them of their sins —

unless they have a mind to repent — and the mulatto child's face is a standing accusation against him who is master and father to the child. What is still worse, perhaps, such a child is a constant offense to the wife. She hates its very presence, and when a slaveholding woman hates, she wants not means [she doesn't lack methods] to give that hate telling effect. Women white women, I mean, — are IDOLS at the south, not WIVES, for the slave women are preferred in many instances; and if these idols but nod or lift a finger, woe to the poor victim: kicks, cuffs, and stripes are sure to follow.

Masters are frequently compelled to sell this class of their slaves out of deference to the feelings of their white wives; and shocking and scandalous as it may seem for a man to sell his own blood to the traffickers in human flesh, it is often an act of humanity toward the slave-child to be thus removed from his merciless tormentors. I was regarded as fair-looking for one of my races, and for four years, a white man — I spare the world his name had base designs upon me. I do not care to dwell upon this subject, for it is one that is fraught with pain. Suffice it to say that he persecuted me for four years, and I— I— became a mother. The child of which he was the father was the only child that I ever brought into the world. If my poor boy ever suffered any humiliating pangs on account of birth, he could not blame his mother, for God knows that she did not wish to give him life. He must blame the edicts of that society which deemed it no crime to undermine girls' virtue in my then position.

ELIZABETH KECKLEY, Behind the Scenes: Or, Thirty Years a Slave, and Four Years in the White House, 1868

The slave traders would buy young and able farm men and well-developed young girls with fine physique to barter and sell. They would bring them to the taverns where there would be the buyers and traders, display them and offer them for sale. At one of these gatherings, a colored girl, a mulatto of fine stature and good looks, was put on sale. She was of high spirits and determined disposition. At night she was taken by the trader to his room to satisfy his bestial nature. She could not be coerced or forced, so she was attacked by him. In the struggle, she grabbed a knife, and with it, she sterilized him, and from the result of injury, he died the next day. She was charged with murder. Gen. Butler, hearing of it, sent troops to Charles County [Maryland] to protect her, they brought her to Baltimore, later she was taken to Washington where she was set free. . . This attack resulted from being good-looking, for which many a poor girl in Charles County paid the price. There are several cases I could mention, but they are distasteful to me.

There was a doctor in the neighborhood who bought a girl and installed her on the place for his own use, his wife, hearing it, severely beat her. One day her little child was playing in the yard. It fell head down in a post hole filled with water and drowned. His wife left him; afterward, she said it was an affliction put on her husband for his sins.

Let me explain to you very plain without prejudice one way or the other, I have had many opportunities, a chance to watch white men and women in my long career, colored women have many hard battles to fight to protect themselves from assault by employers, white male servants or by white men, many times not being able to protect [themselves], in fear of losing their positions. Then, on the other hand, they were subjected to many impositions by the women of the household through woman's jealousy.

RICHARD MACKS, enslaved in Maryland, interviewed 1937 [WPA Slave Narrative Project]

One time dey sent me on Ol' man Mack Williams' farm here in Jasper County [Georgia]. Dat man would kill you sho. If dat little branch on his plantation could talk, it would tell many a tale 'bout folks bein' knocked in de head. I done seen Mack Williams kill folks, an' I done seen 'im have folks killed. One day he tol' me dat if my wife had been good lookin', I never would sleep wid her agin 'cause he'd kill me an' take her an' raise chilluns off'n her. Dcy uster [used to] take women away fum dere husbands an' put wid some other man to breed jes' like dey would do cattle. Dey always kept a man penned up, an' dey used 'im like a stud hoss.

WILLIAM WARD, enslaved in Georgia, interviewed 1937 [WPA Slave Narrative Project]

Durin' slavery if one marster had a big boy en' nuther had a big gal de marsters made dem libe tergedder. Ef'n de' oman didn't hab any chilluns, she wuz put on de block en sold en' nuther' oman bought. You see dey raised de chilluns ter mek money on jes lak we raise pigs ter sell.

SYLVIA WATKINS, enslaved in Tennessee, interviewed ca. 1937 [WPA Slave Narrative Project]

I 'member he had a real pretty gal on his place. . . One of the overseers was crazy about her, but her mother had told her not to let any of 'em go with her. So this old overseer would stick close 'round her when they was workin', just so he could get a chance to say somethin' to her. He kept followin' this child and followin' this child until she almost went crazy. Way afterwhile she run away and come to our house and and stayed 'bout three days. When my marster found out she was there, he told her she would have to go back, or at least she would have to leave his place. He didn't want no trouble with nobody. When that child left us, she stayed in the woods until she got so hungry she just had to go back. This old man was mad with her for leavin', and one day while she was in the field, he started at her again, and she told him flat-footed she warn't goin' with him he took the big end of his cow hide and struck her in the back so hard it knocked her plumb crazy. It was a big lake of water about ten yards in front of 'em, and if her mother hadn't run and caught her, she would have walked right in it and drowned.

In them, times white men went with colored gals and women bold[ly]. Any time they saw one and wanted her, she had to go with him, and his wife didn't say nothin' 'bout it. Not only the men but the women went with colored men too. That's why so many women slave owners wouldn't marry, 'cause they was goin' with one of their slaves. These things that's goin' on now ain't new; they been happenin'. That's why I say you just as well leave 'em alone 'cause they gwine [going] to do what they want to anyhow.

Now sometimes, if you was a real pretty young gal, somebody would buy you without knowin' anythin' 'bout you, just for yourself.

Before my old marster died, he had a pretty gal he was goin' withand he wouldn't let her work nowhere but, in the house, and his wife nor nobody else didn't say nothin' 'bout it; they knowed better. She had three chillun for him, and when he died, his brother come and got the gal and the chillun.

One white lady that lived near us at McBean slipped in a colored gal's room and cut her baby's head clean off 'cause it belonged to her husband. He beat her 'bout it and started to kill her, but she begged, so I reckon he got to feelin' sorry for her. But he kept goin' with the colored gal, and they had more chillun.

Unnamed former slave, enslaved in Georgia, interviewed ca. 1937 [WPA Slave Narrative Project]

Dey lots of places where de young massas has heirs by nigger gals. Dey sell dem jes' like other slaves. Dat purty common. It seem like de white women don't mind. Dey didn't' ject [object], 'cause dat mean more slaves.

CHRIS FRANKLIN, enslaved in Louisiana, interviewed ca. 1937 [WPA Slave Narrative Project]

On this plantation were more than 100 slaves who were mated indiscriminately and without any regard for family unions. If their master thought that a certain man and woman might have strong, healthy offspring, he forced them to have sexual relation, even though they were married to other slaves. If there seemed to be any slight reluctance on the part of either of the unfortunate ones, "Big Jim" would make them consummate this relationship in his presence. He used the same procedure if he thought a particular couple was not producing children fast enough. He enjoyed these orgies very much and often entertained his friends in this manner; quite often, he and his guests would engage in these debaucheries, choosing for themselves the prettiest of the young women. Sometimes they forced their victims' unhappy husbands and lovers to look on.

Louisa and Sam were married in a very revolting manner. To quote [Louisa]: "Marse Jim called me and Sam ter him and ordered Sam to pull off his shirt — that was all the McClain niggers wore —, and he said to me: Nor, 'do you think you can stand this big nigger?' He had that old bull whip flung acrost his shoulder, and Lawd, that man could hit so hard!

So, I jes said 'yassur, I guess so,' and tried to hide my face so I couldn't see Sam's nakedness, but he made me look at him anyhow."

"Well, he told us what we must git busy and do in his presence, and we had to do it. After that, we were considered man and wife. Me and Sam was a healthy pair and had fine, big babies, so I never had another man forced on me, thank God. Sam was kind to me, and I learnt to love him."

SAM & LOUISA EVERETT, enslaved in Virginia, interviewed in 1936 [WPA Slave Narrative Project]

So, we see with these slave narratives, these first-hand accounts of ex-slaves and fugitive slaves, that their slaveholders raped women, forced women and men to have sex with each other, beat women because they didn't want to have sex with them, and made whatever slave (women and man) they thought was strong to sleep with each other to have stronger offspring's. There are more narratives of ex-slaves I could have shared, but this should be enough. The information about these narratives came from the National Humanities Center Resource Toolbox, The Making of African American Identity: Vol. I, 1500-1865. Slavery came with so many awful practices surrounding sex, and the paranoia of Africans being over sexually and unable to control their beastly nature was not the Africans but the Arabs but especially the Europeans because they created many theories; to justify these wicked practices within slavery. One of the theories is the "Mandingo Theory," in the next chapter; I will discuss that.

Chapter V
Mandingo Theory

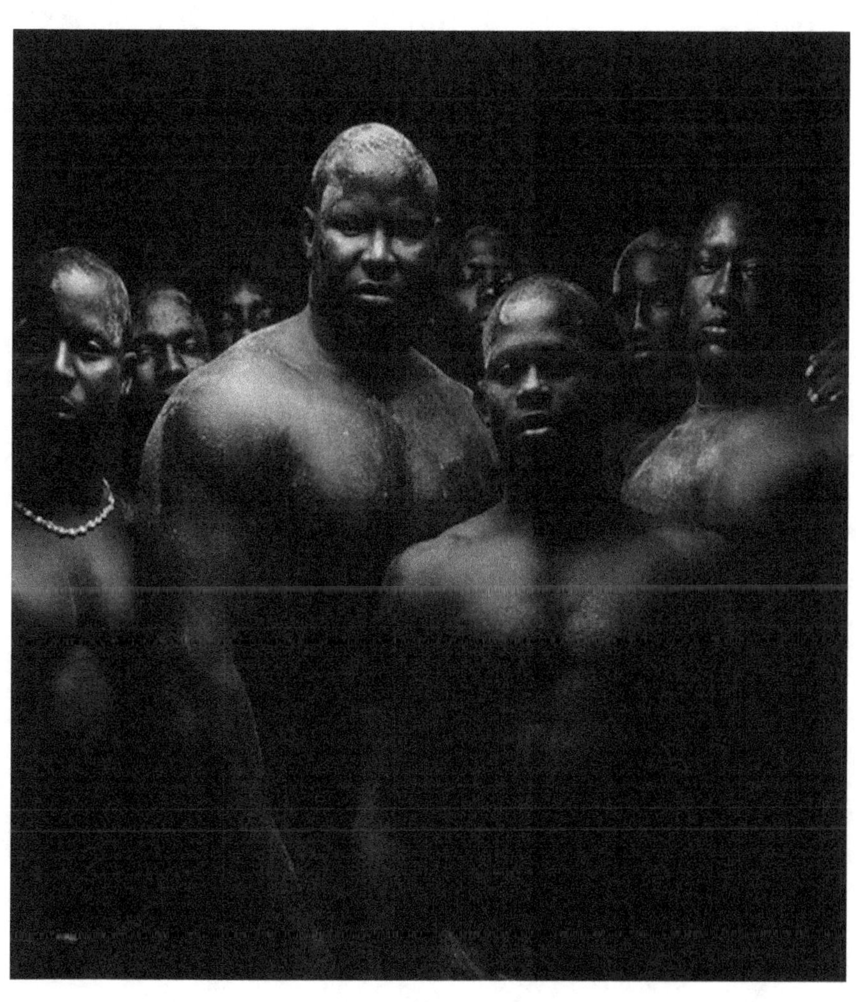

Mandingo Theory

What are the origin and the meaning of the word Mandingo? There is two different meaning, and a straightforward definition is Mandingo is a member of a people of western Africa in or near the upper Niger Valley, and the other is a sexually active African American male with a large penis. One origin is in Africa, and the other origin is in America, which has become a stereotype.

According to British explorer, botanist Henry Hamilton Johnston, and author Frank R. Cana MANDINGO is the name currently given to a significant division of negro peoples in West Africa. It is seemingly a corruption of a term applied to an essential section of this group, the Mande-nka or Mande-nga. The present writer has usually heard this word pronounced by the Mandingo themselves "Mandiña," or even "Madiña." It seems to be derived from the racial name Mande, coupled with the suffix nka or nke, meaning "people," the people of

Mande. Then again, this word Mande seems to take the varying forms of Male, Meli, Mane, Madi, and, according to such authorities as Binger, Delafosse, and Desplagnes, it is connected with the word Mali, which means "hippopotamus" or else "manati"—probably the latter. According to Desplagnes, the term is further divisible into ma, which would have meant "fish," and nde, a syllable to which he ascribes the meaning of "father." In no Mandingo dialect known to the present writer (or in any other known African language) does the vocable ma apply to "fish," and in only one very doubtful far eastern Mandingo dialect is the root nde or any other similar sound applied to "father." This etymology must be abandoned, probably in favor of Mani, Mali, Madi, Mande, meaning "hippopotamus," and in some cases, the other big water mammal, the manati.

Captain L. G. Binger, Du Niger au Golfe de Guinee, &c. (1892)

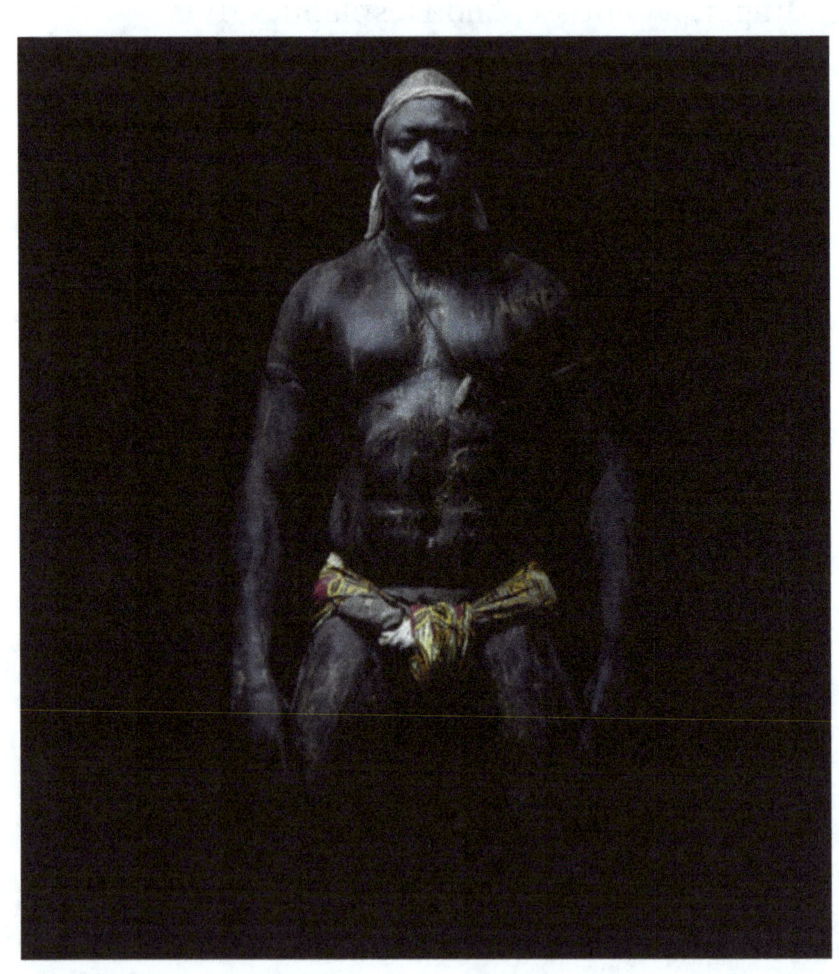

Who are the Mandinka/Mandingo people?

The Mandinka, also known as the Mandingo or Malinke, is one of the largest and most popular ethnic groups in West Africa. They have an estimated population of over 11 million across the West African region. While the Mandinka people can be found in Guinea Bissau, Mali, Sierra Leone, Cote d'Ivoire, Senegal, Burkina Faso, Liberia, Niger, Mauritania, and Chad, the majority of them live in the Gambia. They are descendants of the Mali Empire that rose to power under the rule of the great king Sundiata Keita. They make up one of the largest ethnolinguistic groups called the Mande, which numbers more than 20 million people, including the Dyula, Bozo, and Bambara.

Why Study - National African Language Resource Center. https://nalrc.indiana.edu/doc/brochures/mandinka.pdf.

Primarily the Mandingo people centered on agriculture; Mandinka/Mandingo villages are ruled by local chiefs and a select group of elders. While many today live in big cities where modern dress styles are common, in local villages, there is great pride in maintaining long-standing traditions and forms of dress. In many West African countries, women generally wear a loose, scoop-necked top over long skirts with an accompanying headwrap. For formal occasions, men and women may wear the grand boubou. For women, this is a loose dress that extends to ground level and may be trimmed in lace or embroidery. For men, it is a long robe-like garment covering long pants and a shirt.

While many members of the Mandinka contribute to the larger community as farmers, another large portion are traditional artists, musicians, craftsmen, and athletes. "Laamb" or traditional hand-to-hand combat wrestling, is a prevalent sport both in Gambia and Senegal. As in many sports, the men who participate take on a great undertaking in training and are highly revered. Traditionally, young men also used the sport to court wives, prove manliness, and bring honor to their villages. Oils are spread across the body during pre-fight rituals, and amulets are placed around their necks for protection against evil or witchcraft.

Regarding the arts, music and mask making are most prominent. Well known for their skill in passing down their oral history, the Mandinka are also well known for their mask-making skill. Often masks depict the faces of warriors, as this tribe is known for its brave fighters and fighting style. Interestingly in connection with the arts, it is said that quite a few of today's African American descendants living in America today descended from the people of the Mandinka. If this is true, it is no wonder the strength and power of music / the arts have survived in its black American descendants, the creators of the most influential form of music today ... hip-hop!

Barimah, Angela Adwoa. The Mandinka / Mandingo Tribe. Queen Adwoa's Closet, 2019.

Speaking of hip-hop, the Philadelphia rap artist Black Thought from the legendary hip-hop did a DNA analysis, revealing that his ancestry goes back to Sierra Leone and Senegal. In an interview with bandmate Questlove, Black Thought proudly said he is Mandingo. He said he had no clue of where he was from in Africa before he took a DNA test, but if he had to guess, he would be Mandingo, and it turns out he was right. His bandmate Questlove also took DNA analysis, and his ancestry refers back to Sierra Leone in West Africa.

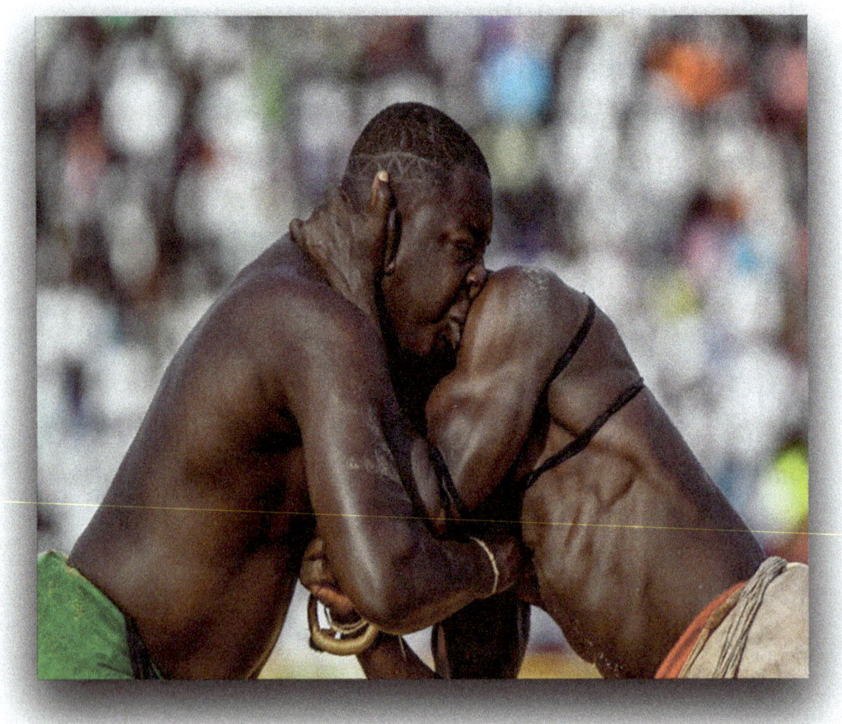

Mandingo wrestling in Senegal

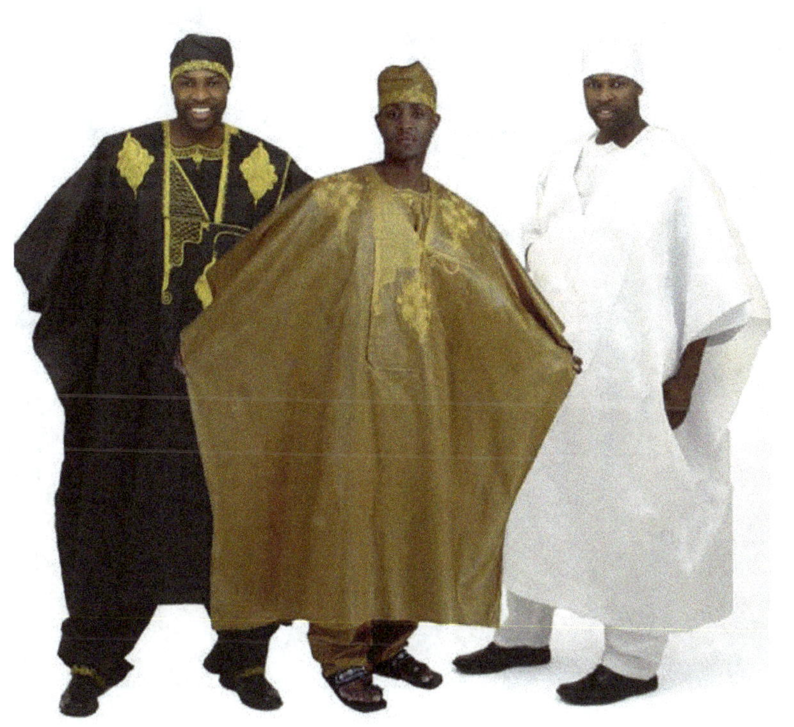

Men boubou-traditional-clothing

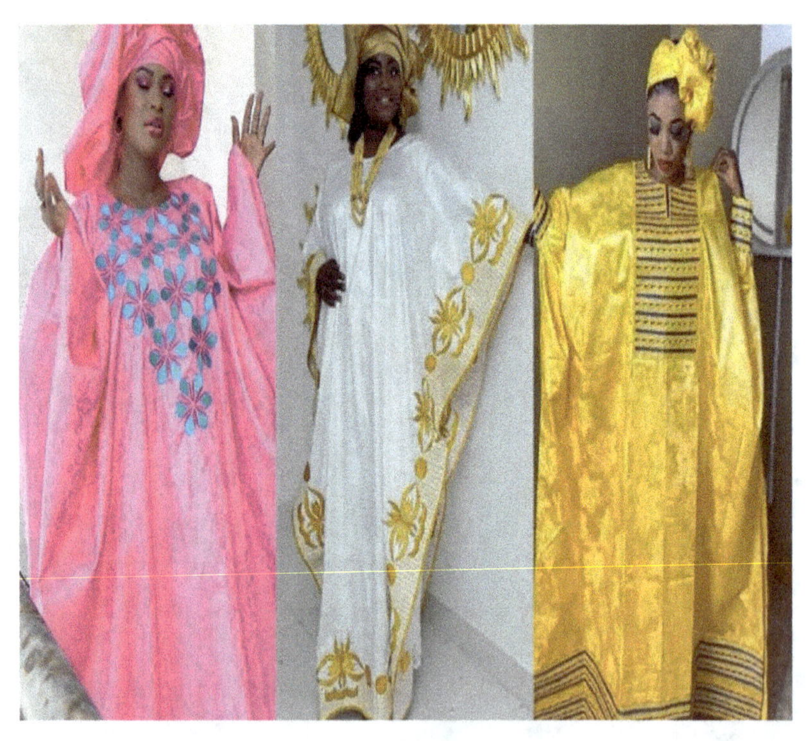

Women boubou-traditional-clothing

On the first page of this chapter, I mention that Mandingo has two different meanings, and when the word reaches America, it becomes negative and a stereotype. Jezebel is negative and stereotype referring to African women.

Mandingo

The Mandingo is a stereotype of a sexually voracious black man with a huge penis, invented by white slave owners to promote the notion that blacks were not civilizable but "animalistic" by nature. They asserted, for example, that in "Negroes all the passions, emotions, and ambitions, are almost wholly subservient to the sexual instinct" and "this construction of the oversexed black male parlayed perfectly into notions of black bestiality and primitivism.

Davis, Gary L.; Cross, Herbert J. (1979). "Sexual stereotyping of Black males in interracial sex." Archives of Sexual Behavior

Jezebel

The Jezebel, a stereotype of a sexually voracious, promiscuous black woman, was the counter-image of the demure Victorian lady in every way. The idea stemmed from Europeans' first encounter with seminude women in tropical Africa. The African practice of polygamy was attributed to uncontrolled lust, and tribal dances were construed as pagan orgies, in contrast to European Christian chastity.

White, Deborah Gray (1999). Ar'n't I a Woman. W. W. Norton & Company.

The supposed indiscriminate sexual appetite of black women slaves justified their enslavers' efforts to breed them with other slaves. It also justified rape by white men, even as a legal defense. Black women could not be rape victims because they "always desired sex." The abolitionist James Redpath wrote that slave women were "gratified by the criminal advances of Saxons." During and after Reconstruction, "Black women... had little legal recourse when raped by white men, and many Black women were reluctant to report their sexual victimization by Black men for fear that the Black men would be lynched.

Leiter, Andrew (2010). In the Shadow of the Black Beast. LSU Press. pp. 176, 38, 220, 4, 33.

Those European powers would come up with anything to justify their evil doing. They believed African males were over-sexual and couldn't help themselves, so they feared the African man raping their white women. They castrated them but made it okay for them (Europeans) to rape the African women because they had a big sexual appetite. All of this was untrue and was drawn up in the minds of the Europeans. I will keep repeatedly reiterating the European's belief, lies, and false justification.

Mandingo Theory Originated from White Slave Owners

The history of black male castration arose within the social framework of power and subordination. In particular, white male domination and control, in many ways, remained contingent upon black male subordination. Predating the slavery era, whites portrayed people of African descent as primitive and animalistic as part of the process of demonizing African men. This animalistic conceptualization naturally led to stereotyping black men as both hypersexual and hyperaggressive "in the Negro, all the passions, emotions, and ambitions, are almost wholly subservient to the sexual instinct."

At the core, this construction of the oversexed black male parlayed perfectly into notions of black bestiality and primitivism. Whites framed black male sexuality in a manner that evoked connotations of the "foreign," "imposing," and "unnatural." Within American society, black males thus emerged as the sexualized Other. When these sex-crazed conceptualizations of black men juxtaposed themselves against the countervailing white women as pure and docile, the stage was set for interracial tension and conflict.

Richeson , Marques P. Sex, Drugs and Race to Castration: Black Box Warning of Chemical Castration . Harvardblackletter, 2009.

Indeed, while the rape of black women was legal, American political and judicial institutions provided excessive protections for white women, crafting a regime of racialized property. The white male preoccupation with the sexual activity of white women, however, found its roots as much in fear as in love. Driven by fear of black male sexuality, the law of sexual assault and rape emerged as a tool to fortify white male power and control over their possessions – black women and white women. By constructing myths concerning the sanctity, chastity, and purity of white womanhood, moreover, white men firmly established white women as a protected property interest.

The ensuing property-based struggle dictated the sway of interracial relations within American society. As the rightful "owners" of white women, white men ascertained a need to protect white women from savage and rapacious black men attempting to "steal" them. Earl Hutchinson, the author of The

Assassination of the Black Male Image, defined the “Big Black Scare” as the societal perception of a widespread black male conspiracy to acquire land, power, and white women. This fear was, in part, reinforced by the purported sexual prowess of black men, the Mandingo Theory.

Richeson , Marques P. Sex, Drugs and Race to Castration: Black Box Warning of Chemical Castration . Harvardblackletter, 2009.

Mandingo theory

Such societal preconceptions by the majority of the white community gave birth to and further reinforced the 'Mandingo theory' which to several attempts by many doctors and pseudoscientists to "deemphasize the gravitational force of the Mandingo obsession by advancing theories that the larger genitalia coincided with a smaller brain, lower intellectual endowment, and increased lasciviousness such efforts floundered.

Rumors of black male sexual prowess continued to stimulate and intimidate the imaginations of white America.

Henry Havelock Ellis, a sexual psychologist, noted:

> I am informed that the sexual power of Negroes is the cause of the favor with which they are viewed by some white women of strong sexual passions in America and by many prostitutes. At one time, there was a particular house in New York City to which white women resorted for these "buck lovers." The women came heavily veiled and would inspect the penises of the men before making the selection.

J.A. Rodgers, supra note 44, at 148 (quoting Havelock Ellis' Studies in the Psychology of Sex, Vol. 3, 238)

White male fear of interracial sexual relations impeded the passage of anti-miscegenation laws in many states that prohibited interracial marriage. White liberals and conservatives set their differences aside to support these suppressive regimes of racial segregation. During the nineteenth century, thirty-eight states adopted anti-miscegenation statutes.

The United States Supreme Court upheld the constitutionality of anti-miscegenation laws, moreover, in the 1883 Pace v. Alabama case. In Pace, the Supreme Court ruled that the Alabama anti-miscegenation statute did not violate the Fourteenth Amendment because the statute treated the races equally insofar as whites and blacks were punished equally for breaking the law against interracial marriage and interracial sex. The Pace decision remained good law until it was overturned in 1967 when the Supreme Court unanimously held in Loving v. Virginia that anti-miscegenation laws were unconstitutional.

Surviving until 1967, the long-standing prohibition of interracial marriage contracts in many states reflected a legal reaction to fears of race-mixing. Illustrating the depth of white male fears concerning race-mixing, the scope of anti-miscegenation statutes sometimes branched beyond marriage into the prohibition of mere interracial sex or cohabitation. As late as 1964, for example, a Florida statute stated that:

> Any negro man and white woman, or any white man and negro woman, who are not married to each other, who shall habitually live in and occupy in the nighttime the same room shall be punished by imprisonment not exceeding twelve months, or by fine not exceeding five hundred dollars.

FLA. STAT. ANN. § 798.05 (1964); see also McLaughlin v. Florida, 379 U.S. 184, 184-85(1964) (holding the Florida statute invalid as a denial of equal protection under the Fourteenth Amendment).

This statute exemplified the deep-seeded societal aversion to the notion of sexual relations between black men and white women. Such sentiments, moreover, remained prevalent throughout the twentieth century. When Gunnar Myrdal formulated "The Rank Order of Discrimination" in 1944, the "Big Black Scare" mentality still permeated American society. When asking white Southerners to rank the things they thought blacks coveted, they ranked intermarriage and sexual intercourse with whites as the leading desire – ahead of social equality, desegregation, political enfranchisement, legal equality, and economic opportunity.

Manifesting the paranoia of the "Big Black Scare," many whites believed that the black male desire for interracial sexual intercourse was so strong that black men would go to any extent, including rape, to satisfy their savage desires. For example, Iwan Bloch, a noted early sexologist, hypothesized that the desire of blacks to mate with whites was much greater than that of whites to mate with blacks. He stated:

> "Much greater is the alluring force exercised by the white upon the black; more especially among the civilized Negroes does the white woman play the part of a fetish. This is the explanation of the frequent rape or attempted rape on white girls on the part of Negroes – one of the principal causes of the Southern lynchings."

Wan Bloch, Sexual Life of Our Time In Its Relations to Modern Civilization 614 (1908)

This call so calls German sexologist Iwan Bloch was way off. He says that the desire of Africans to mate with Europeans was higher than the European wanting to mate with Africans. Ok, now we look at the historical record of the Trans-Atlantic slave trade; the

Europeans have all forced their way on our women sexually. The European man has also forced himself on the African man, but this is taboo and not spoken about; the European woman has also forced her way on the African man, which we do not hear much about. In the next chapter, I will talk about the European woman forcing the African man to have sex with her and how it looks upon by European slaver holder wives to have sex and a child with African slaves. The very idea of the Mandingo Theory or theories was formed in the head of the Europeans, and these theories gave them justification for **castration**, **rape**, **sexual abuse**, and **breeding** of Africans. These crimes would further live on even after the slave trade ended.

Chapter VI
Sex Between White Women and African Male Slave

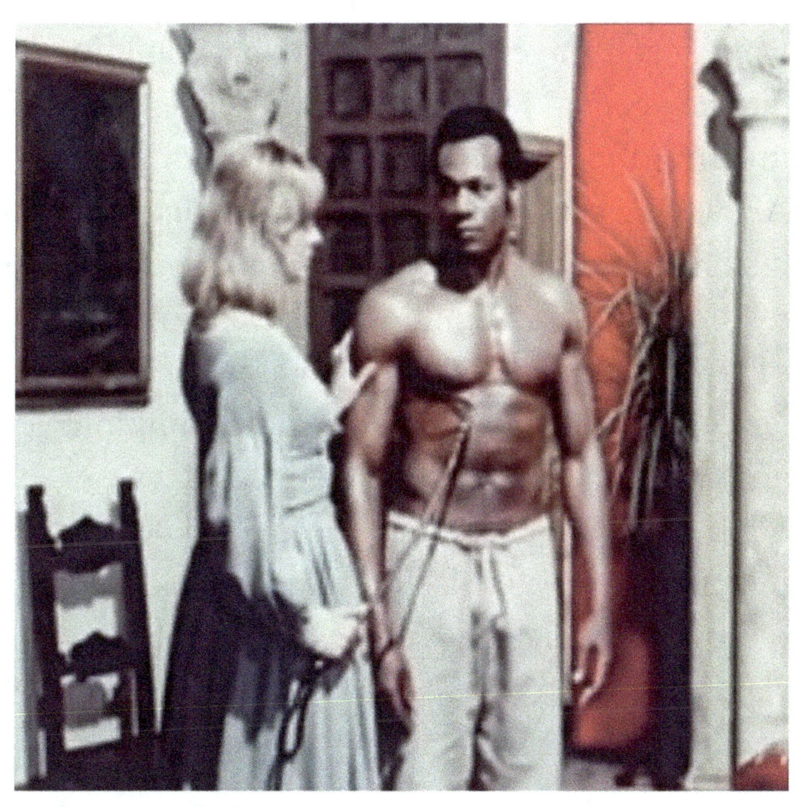

Sex Between White Women and African Male Slave

Sexual relations between planter-class white women and slave men? Under what conditions did they occur? How should they be described in terms of power, agency, and consent? Answering these questions involves analyzing historical records through the lens of power relations and parsing through the complexities of racial, class, and gender hierarchies. By "focusing attention on the ways that multiple and sometimes conflicting sources of oppression and power are intertwined," such an intersectional analysis allows us to make sense of how persons occupying a position of low status in one social arena can simultaneously occupy one of high-status in another.

They also allow us to observe the processes by which social hierarchies are sustained. In the case of white women and black men, we can use an intersectional analysis to understand better how elite Southern white women used oppressive, gendered notions of female purity and sexual subservience to maintain the racial hierarchy.

Aulette , Judy Root, et al. Gendered Worlds. New York : Oxford University Press, 2009.

Reading the first two paragraphs in this chapter, a question and analysis of Judy Root Aulette, Judith G Wittner; Kristin Blakely, who have their Ph.D. in sociologist, and using the skills and tools they were taught to assess why the slaveholder's wives would seek sex with the African slaves, which was forced. African slaves did not want to participate because they feared getting caught by their slaveholders, who would torture and kill them. It is also known in the historical record that if a white woman got caught having sex with an African male, she would scream rape. We already know, reading other chapters in this book the Europeans had already put in their minds that Africans wanted to rape their women to please their over-sexual nature. I will deal more with white women raping African male slaves; yes, I said raping African males for their curiosity and to feel empowered cause we know white men (Europeans) believe they were over the women and their women were inferior to the man.

As guardians of the home, planter-class white women were responsible for upholding traditional Christian values and keeping peace within the domestic sphere. As such, they were valued for their homemaking abilities, maternal instinct, and, perhaps above all else, their virtue. As one letter to a South Carolinian periodical geared toward young women put it,

> If a female possesses beauty, wealth, and, in short, all the accomplishments which wealth can purchase… without VIRTUE, she is "nothing worth." Her accomplishments may be admired by some for a little while, it is true; but she will never be truly esteemed… Permit me to ask, which would you rather have, Virtue without accomplishments or accomplishments without Virtue? (Anonymous, 1832).

Women were seen as physically and intellectually inferior to men but much more pious, pure, and moral (Firor Scott, 1970, 4; Varon, 1998, pp. 10, 13). This trope is expressed by Rev. William Hooper in his 1947 address to the graduating class of the Sedgwick Female Seminary in Raleigh, North Carolina:

> Leave men to themselves without the intermixture of female society and the softening influence of female modesty, gentleness, and affection, and they would infallibly become rude, harsh, coarse, quarrelsome, and in their quarrels, cruel and unrelenting. The world would resemble an amphitheater of wild beasts. Southerners attributed honor and virtue to white women, especially the upper class, "nearly synonymous with a reputation for sexual purity, sustained by restraint, prudence, and modesty in every area of life" (Elder, 2012, pp. 583-84).

White women's sexuality was heavily regulated by law and culture. Adultery was considered a greater offense for women than for men and was punished more harshly. Similarly, "giving birth out of wedlock was... considered much more of a social problem for white women than for anyone else" (Young and Spencer, 2007, p. 69).

The Southern way of life and the institutions that defined it, white supremacy, slavery, and the planter aristocracy were inextricably linked with the sexual regulation of women, especially upper-class women; the purity of white women, when contrasted with the sexually lascivious black Jezebel archetype, served to highlight the alleged superiority of white womanhood, and by extension, whiteness (Brooks Higginbotham, 1992, p. 263).

As historian Catherine Clinton (1982) observes, "If plantation mistresses could live above reproach, their husbands, fathers, sons, and brothers could boast of the superiority of their civilization. The sullying influence of slavery must not touch the women of the upper class lest the entire structure crumbles."

Anon, Anon M. "Sexual Relations between Elite White Women and Enslaved Men in the Antebellum South: A Socio-Historical Analysis." Inquiries Journal, Inquiries Journal, 1 Aug. 2013, http://www.inquiriesjournal.com/articles/1674/sexual-relations-between-elite-white-women-and-enslaved-men-in-the-antebellum-south-a-socio-historical-analysis.

Coupled with the notion of elite white female sexual virtue was that of white female vulnerability, the idea that plantation wives and daughters needed to be protected, defended, and sheltered. Framing women in this way served as a means of patriarchal control. As political scientist Iris Young (2003) explains, "the role of the masculine protector puts those protected, paradigmatically women and children, in a subordinate position of dependence and obedience."

Young, Iris. "Political I Responsibility and Structural Injustice ." Https://Kuscholarworks.ku.edu/Bitstream/Handle/1808/12416/Politicalresponsibilityandstructuralinjustice-2003.Pdf?Sequence=1, 2003.

The United States of America was founded on Christian and Christian morals and accorded to the biblical text, God is above Man, and Man is above women. So, this explains why Europeans consider their women their property. Domestic violence was said to be their method of controlling their wives. Their wives really didn't have freedom and were stuck in the house while their husbands traveled and roam freely. These white women were unhappy with their lack of freedom and their duties to remain please and remain obedient to their husbands while they had affairs raping female African slaves. They couldn't bear looking at their husband's mixed children with the female African slave. This was humiliating and heartbreaking to them. Now, if the slaveholder's woman had an affair with a slave and it was made known as public humiliation. Many times, it was kept silent, and the wife or daughter was sent off until the baby was born and sold.

Southern women, who generally married at a younger age than those in the North, not infrequently at fifteen or sixteen years old (Clinton, pp. 85-86), were often left abandoned on plantations while their husbands traveled for business, pleasure, or military duty (Clinton, p. 103). The life of a plantation mistress was often lonely and sad.

Clinton, Catherine. The Plantation Mistress: Woman's World in the Old South. Pantheon, 1984.

Sex Between White Women and Male Slaves

The fact that affairs between planter-class women and slaves were relatively uncommon is unsurprising; white women in the South were sexually restricted as compared to their male counterparts, and nineteenth-century contraceptive techniques were not nearly effective or accessible enough to ward off the possibility of pregnancy. Still, sexual contact between white women and black men did occur in slaveholding societies, more often than perhaps many are aware. The following is a list of factors that did or may have contributed to the incidence of such relations.

First, even though the sexuality of Southern white women was, as stated, heavily regulated, women were not as entirely sexually repressed as one might assume. According to historian Elizabeth Fox-Genovese (1998), "slaveholding culture emphasized control of female sexuality; it did not deny its existence." She says white women "had a striking lack of neurotic inhibition." Like their husbands, Southern women had pre- and extra-marital sex (though not as often).

Genovese, Elizabeth Fox. "The Pro-Slavery Worldview ." Reviews in American History, vol. 41, 0 Sept. 2013.

Abortion in Nineteenth Century

The dangers of having sexual relations with a black man rather than a white man were enormous in terms of the possibility of producing a mixed-race child. However, although birth control and abortion methods in the nineteenth century were not as widely used, safe, or accessible as they are today, they existed. Condoms made out of animal skin, membrane, oiled silk, and rubber were used along with other contraceptive techniques to prevent pregnancy (Caron, 2008, p. 16).

For much of the nineteenth century, abortion was largely unregulated, and it was not limited to poor, immigrant, or black women; upper- and middle-class white women, too, had abortions (Caron, pp. 22-23). This would have allowed white women to have affairs with black men with some level of confidence that they would not be caught.

Caron, Simone M. Who Chooses? American Reproductive History Since 1830. Florida: University Press of Florida, 2008.

It is also possible that affairs between white women and slaves were simply not noticed or recorded as often as they occurred. While it may have been expected, to a certain extent, that white men would transgress morally (e.g., by having sexual relations with slaves), a white woman choosing to have sex with a black man might not have been considered a likely occurrence.

I find that interesting after reading what Caron Simone says about the slaveholder's wives who would have sex with male African slaves and go get abortions like it wasn't anything. I did not know that this awful practice existed at this time. I did a quick search, nothing in-depth but what I ran across was that this practice of induced abortion, the deliberate termination of a pregnancy, has been known since ancient times. Various methods have been used to perform or attempt abortion, including the administration of abortifacient herbs, the use of sharpened implements, the application of abdominal pressure, and other techniques.

A naturally occurring abortion that ends a pregnancy is sometimes described as "spontaneous" abortion or, with the more frequently used popular euphemism, "miscarriage," to distinguish between induced abortion and a naturally occurring one. Still, medically, abortion is the terminology applied to either natural or induced. It says the first recorded evidence of induced abortion is from the Egyptian Ebers Papyrus in 1550 BCE. Many of the methods employed in early cultures were non-surgical. I am familiar with Ebers Papyrus, and I know it is the oldest and most important medical papyri of ancient Egypt; it was purchased at Luxor in the winter of 1873–74 by Georg Ebers. If my mind serves me right, Eber Payrus was of formals and remedies, and one of the remedies was about birth control. Do your research a verify this information yourself.

An upper-class woman under suspicion of an affair with a slave could "readily invoke images of chastity in order to allay trouble for herself" or in other words, accuse the slave of rape (Hodes, p. 135). Because black men (like black women) were seen as inherently lustful and prone to sexual vice, for an elite woman to have illicit sex with a black rather than a white man might have been a slightly safer bet; it was easier to blame a black man of rape than a white man.

Hodes, Martha. White Women, Black Men: Illicit Sex in the Nineteenth-Century South. New Haven: Yale University Press, 1997.

White women whose affairs with slaves were made known faced varying degrees of public humiliation. When a planter's daughter or wife was discovered to be pregnant by a slave, great pains were taken to cover up the pregnancy. The resulting child might have been sold into slavery, but infanticide was not an uncommon means of avoiding scandal (Hodes, pp. 136-137).

Of course, a scandal was not always avoided. In his 1837 autobiography, former slave Charles Ball describes meeting "the daughter of a wealthy planter, in one of the lower counties of Georgia" who had given birth to a mixed-race son. The family considered sending her out of state until the birth, but instead, "the girl was kept in her father's house, until the birth of her child, which she was not permitted to nurse; it being taken from her." She was "degraded from her rank in society," and her child was sold into slavery.

Sexual Abuse

According to one historian, "few scholars… have viewed the relationships of enslaved men and free white women through the lens of sexual abuse in part because of gendered assumptions about sexual power" (Foster, p. 459). This is in keeping with both the standard feminist conceptualization of rape as a tool of patriarchal oppression3 as well as the traditional (un-feminist) notion of women as too weak, emotionally and physically, to commit serious crimes, let alone sexual abuse, and the idea that men cannot be raped (Bourke, 2007, pp. 219, 328). However, it is becoming increasingly clear that women, too, are capable of committing sexual offenses and using sex as a means of domination and control (Bourke, pp. 209-248).

Indeed, there is considerable documentation of white women coercing black men into having sex. According to Captain Richard J. Hinton, an abolitionist commander in the Civil War, "I have never found a bright-looking colored man, whose confidences I have won… who has not told me of instances where he has been compelled, either by his mistress or by white women of the same class, to have a connection with them" (Hodes, pp. 130-131). One former slave told Hinton that his mistress ordered him to sleep with her after her husband died (Hodes, p. 131). These are just two examples of the many stories abolitionists like Hinton told to prove the immorality of slaveholding.

In Incidents in the Life of a Slave Girl (1867), Jacobs mentions how planters' daughters would take advantage of male slaves:

> They know that the women slaves are subject to their father's authority in all things; and in some cases they exercise the same authority over the men slaves. I have seen the master of such a household whose head was bowed in shame, for it was known in the neighborhood that his daughter had selected one of the meanest slaves on his plantation to be the father of his first grandchild. She did not make her advances to her equals, nor even to her father's more intelligent servants. She selected the most brutalized, over whom her authority could be exercised with less fear of exposure.

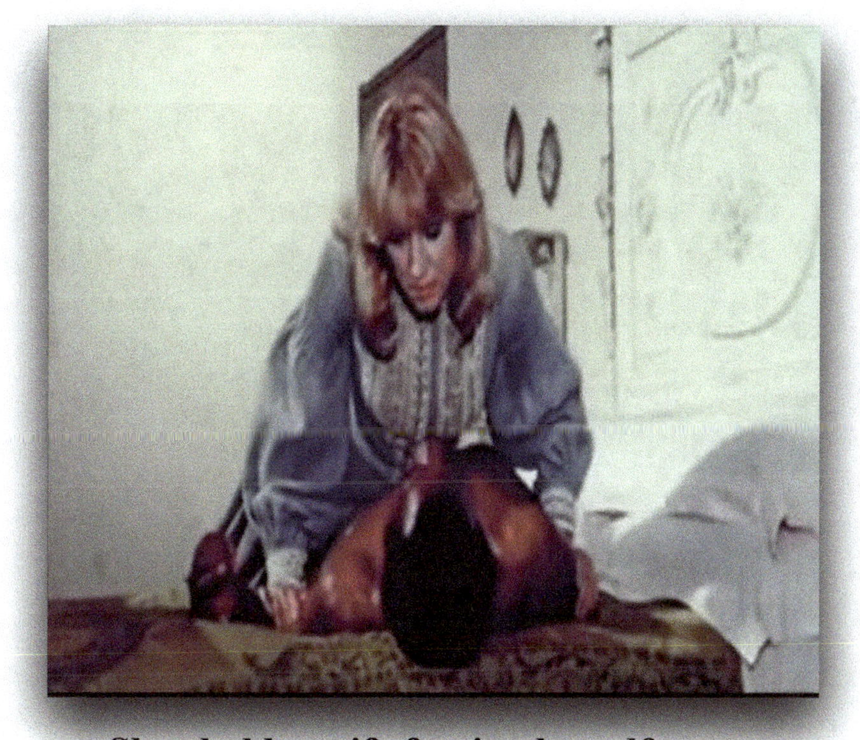

Slaveholder wife forcing herself on an African male slave

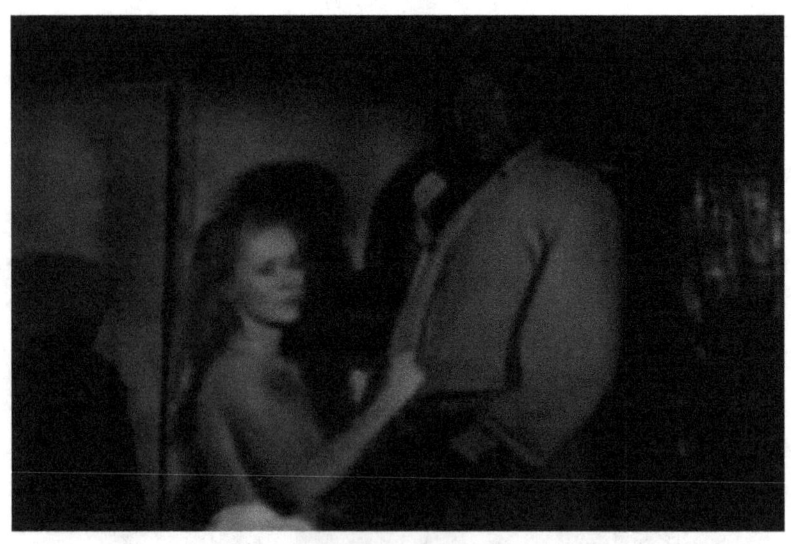

Slaveholder daughter forcing herself on African male slave

Even if the young white woman in this story did not consider herself a sexual assaulter (which she probably did not), this is clearly sexually predatory behavior. The kind of relationship described here, which Jacobs suggests was not uncommon, cannot be classified as consensual in any meaningful sense of the word and constitutes a form of sexual abuse, if not rape. We thus see that plantation mistresses and elite women, like their male counterparts, were able to sexually control and abuse their slaves.

Another way white women could exercise sexual control over slaves was by threatening to accuse them of rape or attempted rape if they did not agree to sex (Hodes, pp. 39, 40, 43, 46, 135). In doing this, elite white women used one of the primary instruments of patriarchal repression—the idea that they were weak and in need of white male protection, and by extension, in need of control and domination by white men—to exercise racial control over slaves. Instead of attempting to dismantle the white patriarchal hegemony that oppressed both slaves and (to a lesser extent) white women, predatory white women who coerced slaves into sex through the threat of rape opted to perpetuate both white supremacy and patriarchy by reinforcing paternalistic notions of female sexuality.

Hodes, Martha. White Women, Black Men: Illicit Sex in the Nineteenth-Century South. New Haven: Yale University Press, 1997.

The white women on these plantations were just as bad as their husbands. They caused havoc on African female slaves that their husband was raping are having an affair with and also caused havoc on those African male slaves by threatening to tell their husband they were trying to rape them if they didn't agree to have sex with them. By them forcing to have their way with the male slave, they feel some sense of power. Getting their desire met because their husbands had their way with their female slaves left them out to be sexually deprived. This was female sexual abuse of slave men. However, just as slave-owning white women often took out their frustrations on slaves through excessive cruelty and violence, they probably also used sex as a means of domination and control in a society in which they were relatively powerless.

The issue of upper-class white female sex with and sexual abuse of male slaves has not received the scholarly attention it deserves. Hodes' White Women, Black Men, is the only book on the subject; most other works on Antebellum slaveholding society either mention it in passing or, like Clinton's The Plantation Mistress, dismiss the possibility of upper-class women having sex with slaves.

Although such relations were rarer than sex between male masters and slave women, they were no less complicated, problematic, and potentially exploitative and no less worthy of scholarly analysis.

Chapter VII
The summary/ Conclusion/My Thought and Opinions

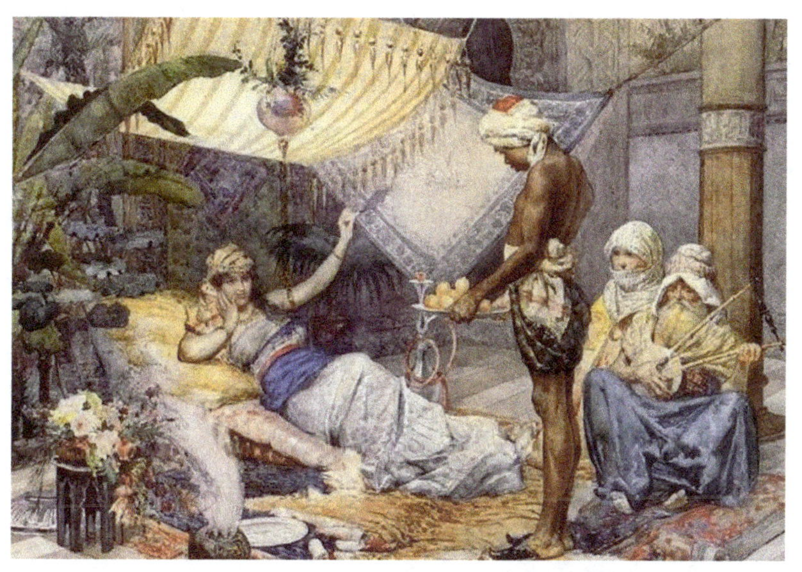

The summary/ Conclusion/My Thought and Opinions

This chapter will consist of a quick summary of each chapter with my thought and opinions on the Trans-Saharan Slave Trade, Trans - Atlantic Slave trade, and the sexual practices in both slave trades. Reading about the crimes within crimes breaks my heart that my people were treated worse than animals.

Slavery what is slavery? Slavery is a condition in which one human being is owned by another. A slave was considered by law as property, or chattel, and was deprived of most of the rights ordinarily held by free persons.

The Arab Muslim slave trade, also known as the trans-Saharan trade or Eastern slave trade, is billed as the longest, having happened for more than 1300 years while taking millions of Africans away from their continent to work in a foreign land in the most inhumane conditions. Male slaves would work as field workers or guards for the harems. To ensure that they never reproduced in case they got intimate with their fellow female slaves, the men and boys were castrated and made eunuchs in a brutal operation where the majority would lose their lives.

The transatlantic slave trade was a maritime trade of African men, women, and children which lasted from the mid-sixteenth century until the 1860s. European traders loaded African captives at dozens of points on the African coast, from Senegambia to Angola and round the Cape to Mozambique. Most captives were collected from West and Central Africa and Angola. The Portuguese and Spanish initiated the trade, and the men and women slaves were worked to death on sugar, crops, tobacco, rice, coffee, cocoa, and cotton plantations for generational wealth.

Castration became a regular practice within Trans-Atlantic Slave Trade because it was believed that castrated boys and men worked faster, were more efficient, and posed no threat. The slave masters could leave them with their families without any fear that they would have affairs with their wives back at home. Remember, the European believed that Africans were over sexually and couldn't help themselves. They believe that their African slaves would rape the so-called pure white women. Castration was also served as punishment.

Sex was also a practice in both slave trades. Arabs had women as sex slaves, and some women rose to have little power. The European rape women and pass them on to their colleagues in their sex games. Seriously African women were forced to have sex with their owners, but their slave owners thought they were doing the female African slaves a favor. White men often claimed they were doing Black women a favor by saving them from having sex with Black men who were considered animalistic and brutal. The white women often beat enslaved women for having sex with their husbands while the husband was never held accountable. Men were also raped by the slaveholder's wives, who were deprived of sex by their husbands. The forcing of the African slaves to have sex with them gave them some sense of power and something to do because their husbands roamed freely and did what they wanted while the wives stayed stuck on the plantations with the slave and overseers.

The European men did not respect their women, ran all over them, and thought their women were also inferior. This is what years later birthed the feminist movement or women's movement by white women. and was later taken over by our women. The movement was in 4 waves, and they were fighting to be treated equally, fighting issues of women's liberation, reproductive rights, domestic violence, maternity leave, equal pay, and women's suffrage. If we look through history, they have never respected their women, and even in their moral compass or guide, which is the bible, they demonized women, and humanity is in sin because of a woman. We have been taught that this is man's world; man is the head of the household, which is rhetoric created by European male chauvinists. We have adopted this way of thinking and begin to treat our women the same in some compacity.

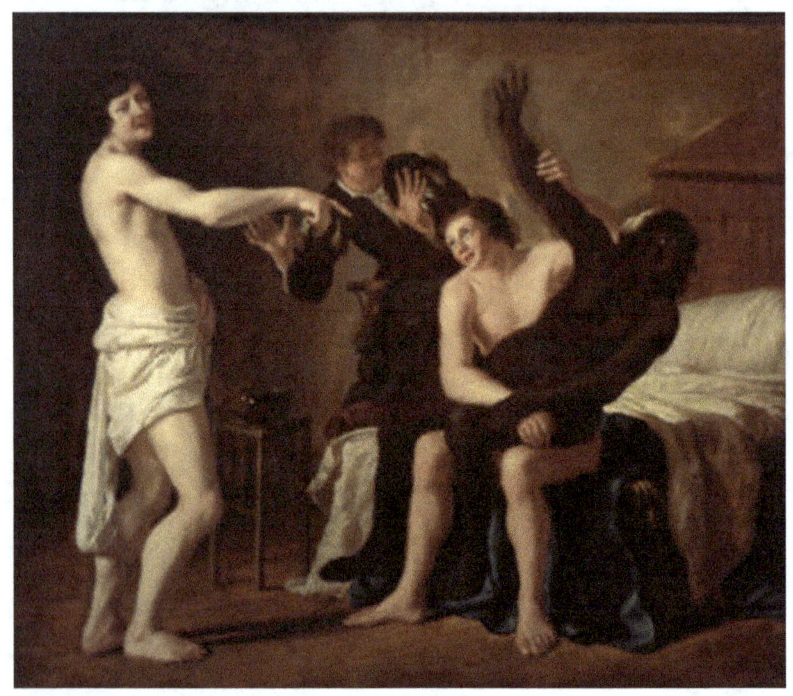

Slave Masters Claimed They Were Doing Black Women A Favor

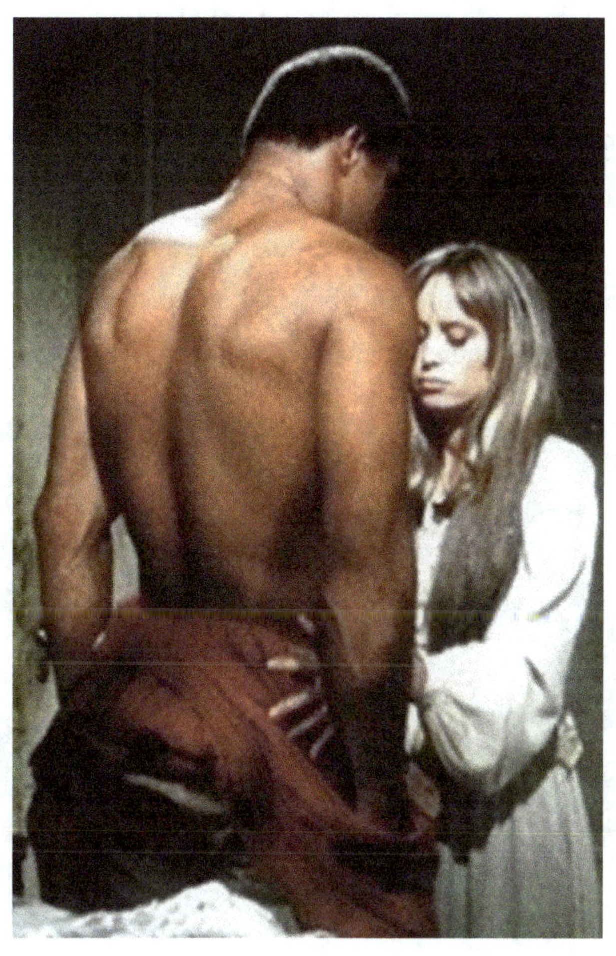

White women forced the male African slave to have sex.

Henry Havelock Ellis, a sexual psychologist, noted:

At one time, there was a special house in New York City to which white women resorted for these 'buck lovers." The women came heavily veiled and would inspect the penises of the men before making the selection. These white women's crimes have not been discussed in my community, only the crimes of their husbands, fathers, and brothers. These white women did as much as their white men.

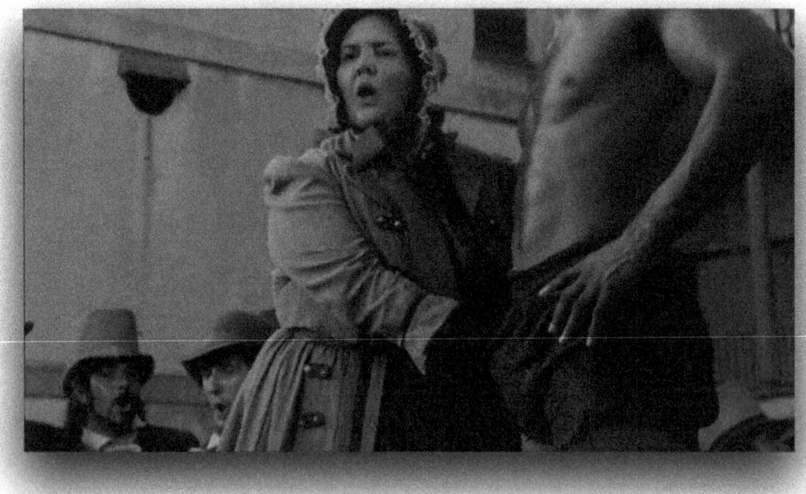

White women or little white girls were gifted slaves by some of their loved ones, not just when their family died. These women starve. Afflicted violence and pain on those African Slaves they were gifted. White women own slaves, and there is limited evidence I came across of how many. These slaves were taken from these young white girls once they got married.

American historian Stephanie E. Jones-Rogers states prevailing scholarship contended that married women rarely possessed control over the property because of a legal doctrine called coverture. Under coverture, when any property-owning or wage-earning woman married, all of her property and wages immediately became her husband's, and he could do whatever he wanted with it. Scholars have looked at this doctrine and, for the most part, argued that these women did not have economic investments in slavery because, by law, their slaves would become their husbands upon marriage.

This was undoubtedly true for some women, but not all of them. Slave ownership allowed these women to exercise certain kinds of power in and over their lives, power and control that would not be available to them if they didn't own enslaved people, and in this way, slavery was their freedom

Castration has existed since ancient times; it started with animals and later with humans. Animal castration has always been ascribed to herd and breeding control, especially for wool herds. Human castration was used for punishment, control, disposal of potential rivals for power, medical 'cures', and the deliberate creation of particular slaves and servants

Castration, according to Arabs, believed it would make them work harder and faster, and unlike the Europeans, the Arabs didn't want their slaves to have sex with the other slaves. Europeans also, in some sense, believed that castrating their slaves would make them work faster.

Still, the key to them practicing castration was due to jealousy, hatred, and paranoia, which developed these theories in their heads. Theories like African men were beast and over sexually, so they couldn't be trusted around their women. Africans wanted interracial sex with white women. An enlarged penis means you have a tiny brain, etc. etc. They use this practice of castration to justify their mandingo theory and just inflict pain on their slaves.

One more thing I would like to touch on before I end this chapter is the Europeans would turn two friends against each other. During the night, they would get a female African slave, her husband, and the husband's friend. Take them to the barn or some location on the plantation grounds and make the female slave have sex with her husband's friend. If the friend refuses, the slave owner or overseers would threaten to castrate him if he didn't do it.

The husband would be forced to watch his wife have sex with his friend. A lot of times, the ones who police the plantation do this and then would instigate for days to the husband how his friend had sex with his wife. This method would turn friends against each other, and at times the results would turn into a fight to the death.

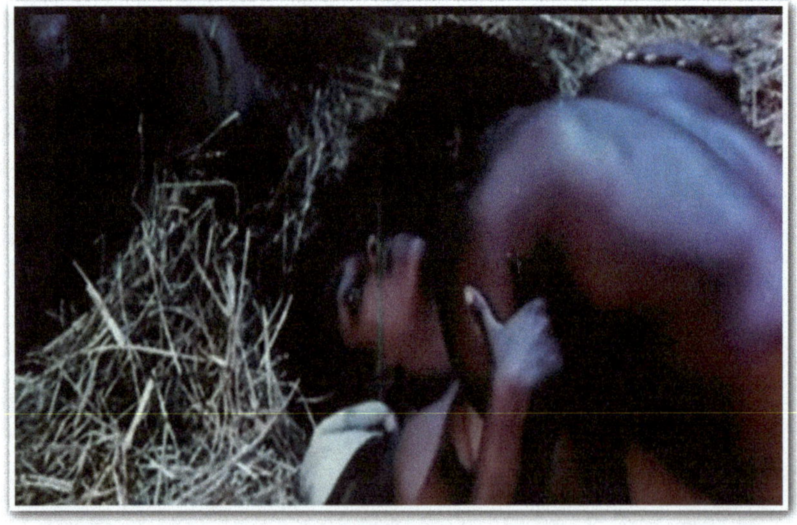

African Slave forced to have sex with his friend's wife

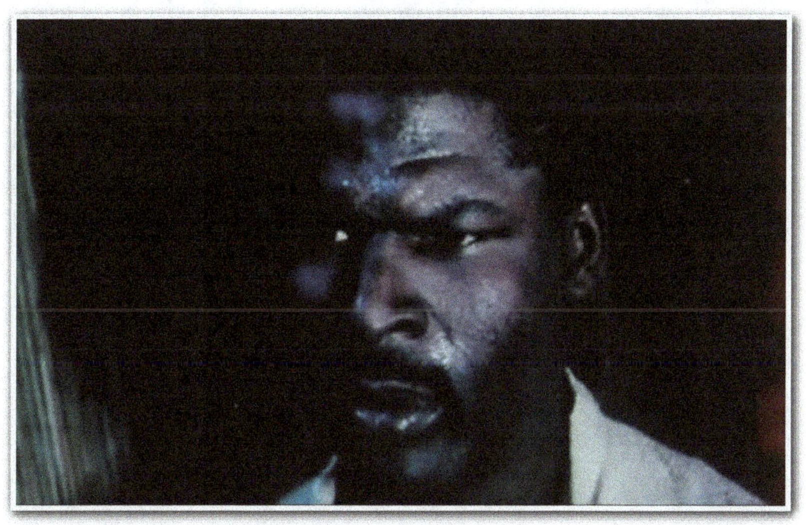

The look on the face of a male slave watching his friend force to have sex with his wife

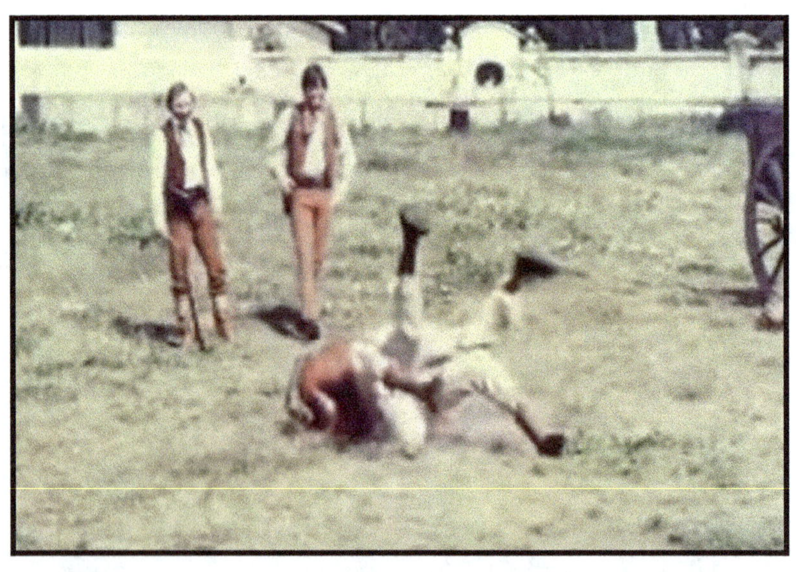

The overseers watch and enjoy the fight they instigated

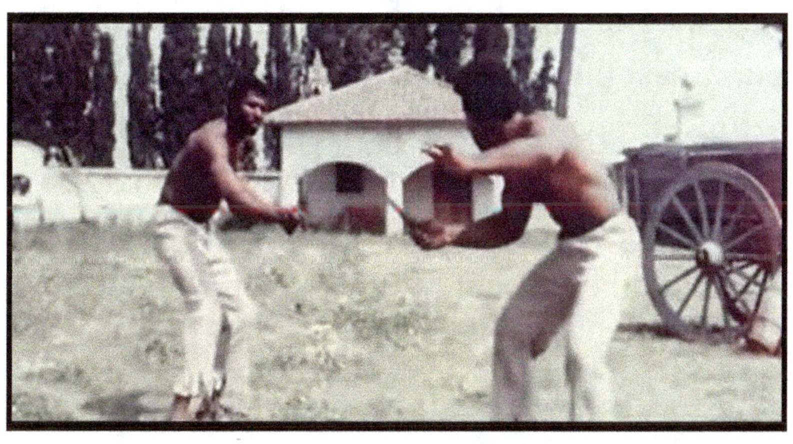

Force to fight to the death

Horrible practices within slavery were immoral and unethical. Europeans were the ones over-sexual and not the Africans. The European man and women couldn't help themselves. The men rape their female slaves, and the women rape the male slaves. They used sex to entertain by passing the female slaves around to have sex with slave owners' friends and colleagues, while the women would also set up a space for other European women to come and inspect the slaves before having sex with them. I wouldn't put it past them that those women were also selling strong Africans or what they would say, Mandingos to other white women to satisfy their sexual needs cause the husband was seeking other sexual favor for their female slaves

Mandingo Theory: Castration of Africans & Sex-crazed Conceptualization was a small presentation. However, after I presented the presentation, I was compelled to do some more research and expand the presentation into a book. This small book touches on the sex-crazed conceptualization of the Arab and the European.

Sex in the Arabs and Europeans slave trade was a tool of power, economics, turning slaves against each other, and pleasure. Sex played a significant role in slavery in many ways.

References

Introduction

· Fatunde, Tunde. "Scholars Focus on the Arab Trans-Saharan Slave Trade." University World News, https://www.universityworldnews.com/post.php?story=20120413180645205

· Nunn, Nathan. Chapter 5. Shackled To The Past: The Causes And Consequences Of Africa's Slave Trades. Aug. 2008, https://scholar.harvard.edu/nunn/files/hup_africa_slave_trade10.pdf.

Chapter One

· Team, Esri's StoryMaps. "Is the World Full or Empty?" ArcGIS StoryMaps, Esri, June 16, 2022, https://storymaps.arcgis.com/stories/b4380439bc8c4293b36a4f9772c665ba.

· Chu, Jennifer (January 2, 2019). "A "pacemaker" for North African climate." MIT News. Retrieved January 20, 2020.

· Cartwright, Mark. "The Salt Trade of Ancient West Africa." World History Encyclopedia, Https://Www.worldhistory.org#Organization, July 24, 2022, https://www.worldhistory.org/article/1342/the-salt-trade-of-ancient-west-africa/.

· The Trans-Saharan Caravan Trade, Religion & Culture. (2015, March 5). Retrieved from https://study.com/academy/lesson/the-trans-saharan-caravan-trade-religion-culture.html.

· McDougall, Ann E. Slavery & Abolition: A Journal of Slave and Post-Slave Studies. n.d.

· Johnson, Elizabeth Ofosuah. "The Chilling Details of the Arab Slave Trade in Africa and the Barbaric Castration of Black Boys." Face2Face Africa, April 6, 2020, https://face2faceafrica.com/article/the-chilling-details-of-the-arab-slave-trade-in-africa-and-the-barbaric-castration-of-black-boys.

· New African. "Recalling Africa's Harrowing Tale of Its First Slavers – The Arabs – as UK Slave Trade Abolition Is Commemorated." New African Magazine, March 27, 2018.

· Preskar, Peter. "The Horrific Medieval Slave Trade Had Gigantic (and Global) Proportions." Medium, History of Yesterday, March 8, 2022, https://historyofyesterday.com/medieval-slave-trade-410725bf9ffe

· Ade, Yewande. "African Male Slaves Experienced Untold Hardship During the Slave Trade Era." History of Yesterday, July 10, 2021.

· Segal, Ronald. Islam's Black Slaves: A History of Africa's Other Black Diaspora. Atlantic Books, 2003

Chapter Two

· Curtis , Perry L., et al. Colonialism in the Congo: Conquest, Conflict, and Commerce. Choices Program, Watson Institute for International Studies, Brown University, 2007.

· Kwekudee. "Pre-Colonial African Kingdom of Kongo: Once a Great Colosus." PRE-COLONIAL AFRICAN KINGDOM OF KONGO: ONCE A GREAT COLOSUS, Blogger, 16 May 2013, https://kwekudee-tripdownmemorylane.blogspot.com/2013/05/pre-colonial-african-kingdom-of-kongo.html

· Mark, Joshua J. "African Slave Life in Colonial British America." World History Encyclopedia, Https://Www.worldhistory.org#Organization, 27 July 2022, https://www.worldhistory.org/article/1732/african-slave-life-in-colonial-british-america/.

· Reiss, O. Blacks in Colonial America. McFarland, 2006.

· Taylor, A. American Colonies: The Settling of North America. Penguin Books, 2002.

Chapter Three

· Martin, Robert D. Unmanned: An Unnatural History of Human Castration. Sussex Publishers, 2016.

· Lohman, Sarah. "A Brief History of Castoreum, the Beaver Butt Secretion Used as Flavoring." Mental Floss, Mental Floss, 13 June 2017, https://www.mentalfloss.com/article/501813/brief-history-castoreum-beaver-butt-secretion-used-flavoring.

· Hopkins, 1978; Kadish, 1969; Ringrose, 1994; Siddall, 2007; Tadmor, 1983

· Reusch, Kathryn. That Which Was Missing: The Archaeology of Castration. University of Oxford, 2013.

· Klaf and Pisetsky, 1962; Millant, 1908

· Kadish, 1969; Kutcher, 2010; Scholz, 2001; Tougher, 2008

· Sima, Qian, et al. War-Lords. Southside, 1976.

Chapter Four

- Sublette, Ned, and Constance Sublette . American Slave Coast: A History of The Slave-Breeding Industry. CHICAGO REVIEW, 2017.

- National Humanities Center on the Masters' Sexual Abuse of Slaves: Selections from 19th- & 20th-c. Slave Narratives

Chapter Five

· Captain L. G. Binger, Du Niger au Golfe de Guinee, &c. (1892)

· Why Study - National African Language Resource Center. https://nalrc.indiana.edu/doc/brochures/mandinka.pdf.

· Barimah, Angela Adwoa. The Mandinka / Mandingo Tribe. Queen Adwoa's Closet, 2019

· Davis, Gary L.; Cross, Herbert J. (1979). "Sexual stereotyping of Black males in interracial sex." Archives of Sexual Behavior

· White, Deborah Gray (1999). Ar'n't I a Woman. W. W. Norton & Company.

· Leiter, Andrew (2010). In the Shadow of the Black Beast. LSU Press. pp. 176, 38, 220, 4, 33.

· Richeson , Marques P. Sex, Drugs and Race to Castration: Black Box Warning of Chemical Castration . Harvardblackletter, 2009.

- J.A. Rodgers, supra note 44, at 148 (quoting Havelock Ellis' Studies in the Psychology of Sex, Vol. 3, 238)

- Wan Bloch, Sexual Life of Our Time In Its Relations to Modern Civilization 614 (1908)

Chapter Six

· Aulette , Judy Root, et al. Gendered Worlds. New York : Oxford University Press, 2009.

· Brooks Higginbotham, 1992, p. 263).

· Anon, Anon M. "Sexual Relations between Elite White Women and Enslaved Men in the Antebellum South: A Socio-Historical Analysis." Inquiries Journal, Inquiries Journal, 1 Aug. 2013, http://www.inquiriesjournal.com/articles/1674/sexual-relations-between-elite-white-women-and-enslaved-men-in-the-antebellum-south-a-socio-historical-analysis.

· Clinton, Catherine. The Plantation Mistress: Woman's World in the Old South. Pantheon, 1984.

· Genovese, Elizabeth Fox. "The Pro-Slavery Worldview ." Reviews in American History, vol. 41, 0 Sept. 2013.

· Hodes, Martha. White Women, Black Men: Illicit Sex in the Nineteenth-Century South. New Haven: Yale University Press, 1997.

Chapter Seven

· Clinton, Catherine. The Plantation Mistress: Woman's World in the Old South. Pantheon, 1984.

Notes

- (Hodes, pp. 136-137).
- (Vintage, 1956), p. 245
- (Elder, 2012, pp. 583-84).
- (Young and Spencer, 2007, p. 69).
- (Brooks Higginbotham, 1992, p. 263).
- (Bourke, pp. 209-248).
- (Bourke, 2007, pp. 219, 328).
- (Caron, pp. 22-23).
- (Clinton, p. 103).

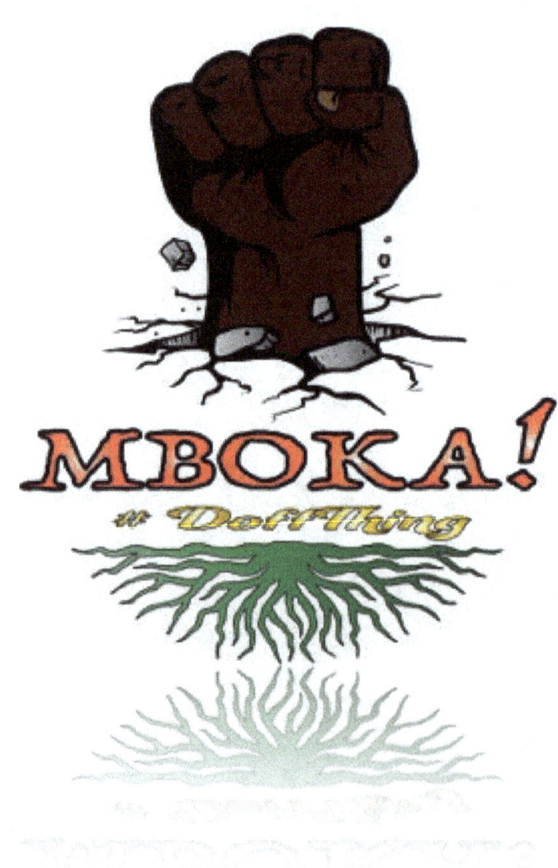
MBOKA!
DefThing

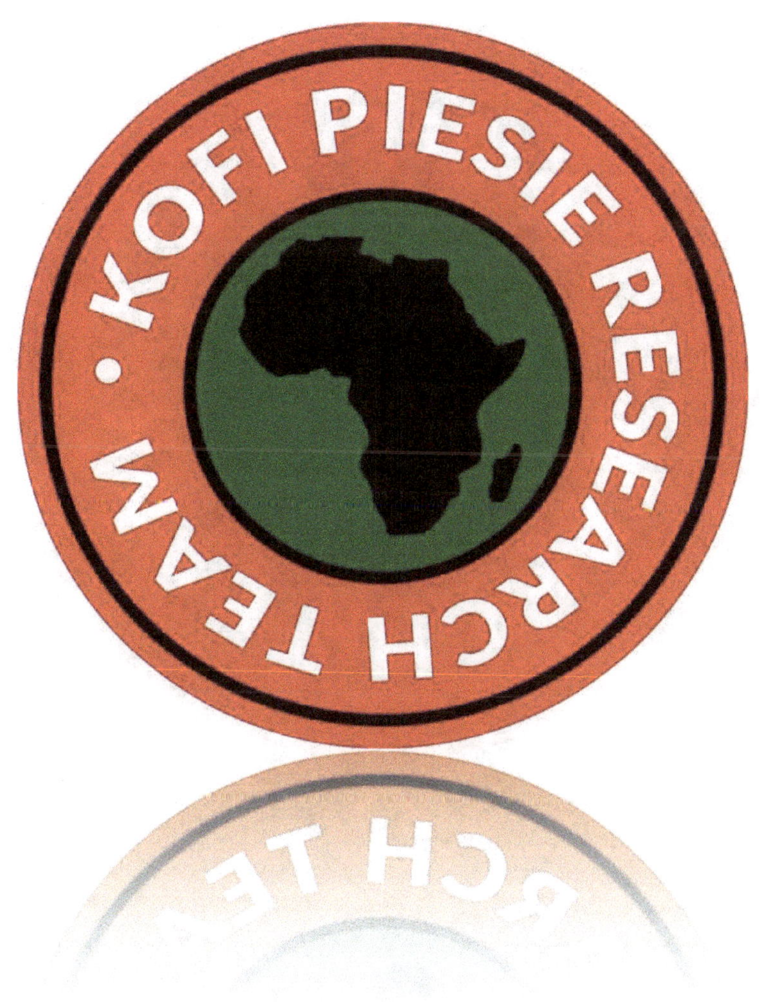
• KOFI PIESIE RESEARCH TEAM

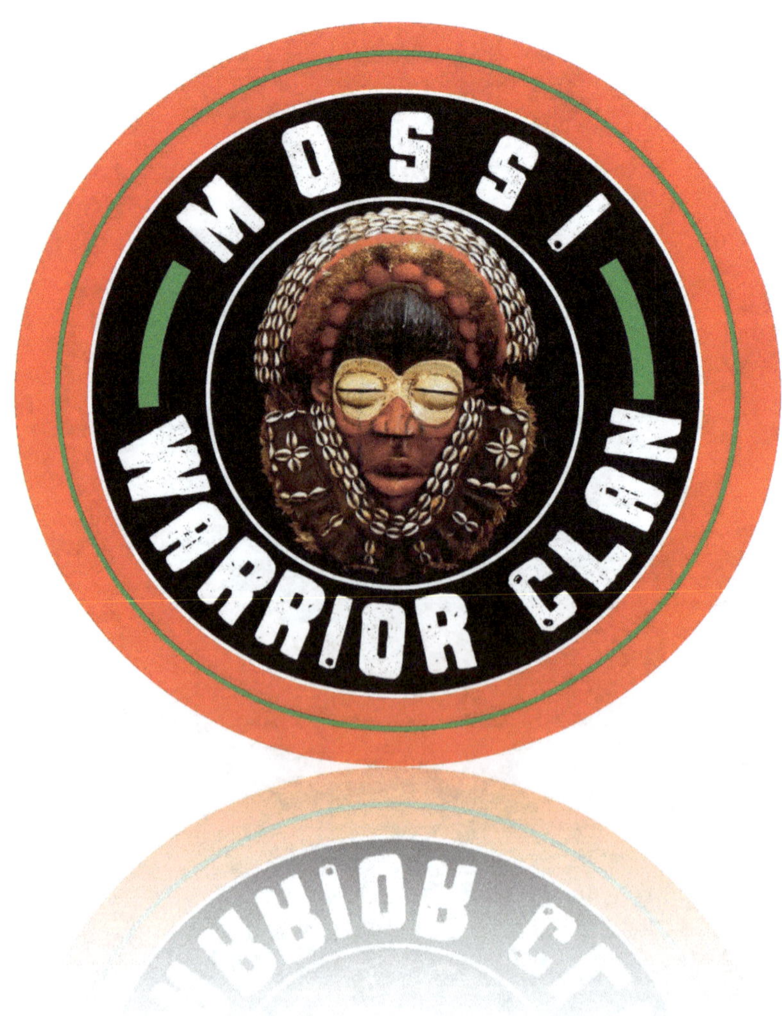
MOSSI
WARRIOR CLAN

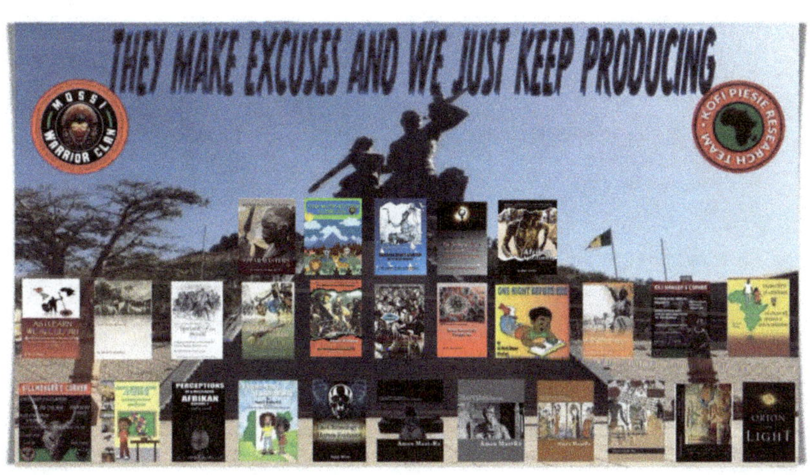
THEY MAKE EXCUSES AND WE JUST KEEP PRODUCING
MOSSI WARRIOR CLAN
KOFI PIESIE RESEARCH TEAM
PERCEPTIONS
AFRIKAN

www.ingramcontent.com/pod-product-compliance
Lightning Source LLC
LaVergne TN
LVHW050534100826
845148LV00002B/555

* 9 7 9 8 9 8 5 1 9 0 9 8 4 *